Andrew Barnes has made a career of market-changing growth and innovation. He was chairman of realestate.com.au (REA Group) at the time of its IPO on the ASX, led the sale of Bestinvest, a US$5.7-billion UK wealth management business, to private capital, and as managing director was instrumental in the creation and listing of Australian Wealth Management Limited on the ASX.

Most recently Andrew triggered a revolution of the entire fiduciary and legal services industries in New Zealand, and his conception of the four-day week – the flexible work revolution – has made him a globally sought-after leader. He speaks to international audiences on the future of work and subjects such as governance, philanthropy, business leadership, entrepreneurship, company culture and change management.

Andrew lives in the United Kingdom and New Zealand. He holds an MA in Law and Archaeology from Selwyn College at the University of Cambridge.

Stephanie Jones is a specialist business writer and non-fiction editor with a background in journalism, magazine publishing and public relations. She holds a BA (Hons) with first-class honours in History and Literature from the University of Auckland.

THE 4 DAY WEEK

How the flexible work revolution can increase productivity, profitability and well-being, and help create a sustainable future

ANDREW BARNES

with Stephanie Jones

piatkus

PIATKUS

First published in Great Britain in 2020 by Piatkus

1 3 5 7 9 10 8 6 4 2

A CIP catalogue record for this book
is available from the British Library.

ISBN: 978-0-349-42490-3

Typeset in Palatino by M Rules
Printed and Bound in the United States at LSC Communications

Papers used by Piatkus are from well-managed forests
and other responsible sources.

Piatkus
An imprint of
Little, Brown Book Group
Carmelite House
50 Victoria Embankment
London EC4Y 0DZ

An Hachette UK Company
www.hachette.co.uk

www.littlebrown.co.uk

*This book is dedicated to my wonderful children,
Genevieve and Sebastian – hopefully they will never have to
work the hours their father did – and to my mother,
Barbara, who always worried about it.*

Contents

'The countries and organizations that can crack the code of the four-day week first could build a competitive advantage, if they can implement it in a way that maximises the well-being benefit on the longer term while minimizing the short-term rise in labour and operational costs.'

Ben Laker and Thomas Roulet
Harvard Business Review, August 2019

The Most Dangerous Man on the Plane

Some 55 years after the US Federal Aviation Administration launched the first in-flight security programme and instigated the practice of populating random flights with highly trained air marshals in civilian garb, a man boards a plane in Auckland, bound for Doha. It is close to Christmas, and warm in the Antipodes, but his final destination is the 4 p.m. winter dusk of London. He carries with him a clean British passport, a laptop and a folder of papers.

Though he is not armed with any conventional weapon, and he slips easily through the scanners with his possessions, he will be the most dangerous passenger on the 17-hour flight. What he does on that plane will generate thousands of news reports and social media posts in dozens of countries in the year after flight QR921 lands in the Qatar capital. As the aircraft touches down, no one yet knows what has been unleashed. Unapprehended, he travels onward.

That man was me. I promise I meant no harm. On the face of it, I had no reason to do what I did. I had lived a good life to that point. I had the privilege of a fine education, first at the University of Cambridge and then at the coalface of global high finance. I had two extraordinary children and an amazingly supportive partner. I was the founder of a thriving trustee company in New Zealand, a country so physically beautiful, culturally diverse and rich with opportunity that anyone who can make a home there has all but won the lottery of life. I could indulge in my pastimes – collecting art, working to restore a classic yacht, growing grapes and making wine on an island in the Hauraki Gulf.

I was all set. Then I disrupted everything.

I boarded the flight with the seemingly innocuous item that would change my life and many others' – an issue of the *Economist* containing a report on two studies of office workers in Canada and the United Kingdom, all of whom worked a stand-ard five-day week. The research found that employees were productive for only 1.5 to 2.5 hours of a typical eight-hour day.

As a business owner responsible for some 240 people, I was gobsmacked. I thought about it and realised that although we did have measurements of output for different roles and busi-ness units, these metrics were by no means ubiquitous, and it was possible – even likely – some of my employees were only productive for a couple of hours a day. I worked out the maths. My theory was if each of my employees was productive for an average of about 2.5 hours per day, then as an employer I only needed to claw back 40 more productive minutes per day to get the same output from staff in a four-day week as in a five-day week. If I succeeded, productivity would remain steady and so would profitability. What I could not predict was how a 'free' day off each week might affect staff well-being and attitudes.

This was the inception of what we now call the 100-80-100 rule. Staff receive 100 per cent of their contractual compensa-tion and need to work only 80 per cent of the time, provided they deliver 100 per cent of the agreed productivity. When I first emailed my human resources director about my brainwave she assumed I was joking, and deleted it. A few weeks later, back in New Zealand, I assured her I was serious, and we set about investigating which leaders had already espoused the benefits of the four-day week. Surely there was nothing new under the sun?

As it transpired, my version of the four-day week was a new idea, as what we were proposing had never been precisely tested. Many companies had experimented with the standard model of full-time work by, for example, compressing forty hours into four days or offering workers reduced hours alongside salary cuts. But the 100-80-100 calculus, with its emphasis on productivity and not just work-life balance, constituted a grand experiment which even most of my own leadership team regarded as impracticable and absurd.

As I explored the four-day week concept further, I was faced with a conundrum: how could we implement a four-day week without significant adverse implications for the business if it went wrong? After all, I had external investors and an independent board of directors who I knew would view the whole idea with a degree of suspicion. It was at that point we decided on a trial of the four-day week, backed up by independent researchers so I had hard evidence to support the validity and viability of the model.

We knew the trial should be of sufficient length to provide good data for the research and our own analysis. Initially we settled upon six weeks, but this was quickly extended to eight weeks as it was felt two full months (and two full processing cycles) would deliver more robust data.

The company's eight-week trial, which was propelled by the goodwill of our staff and tracked diligently by two university researchers, yielded a large pool of data. I became certain of one thing: the five-day week is a nineteenth-century construct that is not fit for purpose in the twenty-first century.

My conviction on that point is the reason I have written this book. I have placed the four-day week in the context of the world of work as it is today. Despite significant technological improvements over the last few decades, the rise of the internet and social media to form a hyperconnected world, and new business models which have disintermediated established companies and industries, there have not been corresponding advances in overall productivity. Equally, while the benefits of these new models are enjoyed by consumers, there has not been a commensurate improvement in the working conditions of employees, with work-related stress swelling to almost epidemic proportions across the whole of the developed and developing worlds.[1]

Of course, I cannot credibly argue that the work conditions of the Fourth Industrial Revolution are more dire than the soot-thickened air of the First, but as the global population grows, the middle class swells and pressure on resources intensifies, there is an urgent need to change – in quite an extreme way – how we work, if we are to get the best out of people and commerce, and begin to relieve the strain on ourselves and our planet.

For those familiar with the four-day week concept, this book presents practical guidelines for its trial and implementation, details the benefits of a productivity-focused, reduced-hour week, and examines the obstacles to its widespread adoption and how we might overcome them.

As for the man on the plane, he is still pinching himself. It is hard to believe that the events of the last year took place. Far from being widely rejected as unfeasible, our four-day week story catalysed one of the most astonishing years of my life, and started a global conversation about the future of work.

It made the agenda at the World Economic Forum in Davos. I found myself a media subject in many countries; in TV interviews by, among others, American, British, Japanese, Ukrainian and French networks, and on radio stations from Canada to South Africa. Traditional and online outlets pounced on the topic, and audiences responded. At one point, the Perpetual Guardian four-day week was the most-read story in the *New York Times* after the Trump/Putin summit.

A simple idea prompted by a news report morphed into a debate that has so far reached people in 75 countries and is gaining traction as dozens of companies stage trials and begin to contribute to the evidence base. Meanwhile, the four-day week is being seriously discussed by governments and policy-makers and has already been adopted by organisations such as the Trades Union Congress and the Green Party and the Labour Party in the United Kingdom. As I write, the Russian Parliament has started to draft legislation for the gradual implementation of a four-day week across the country.

It is very humbling, and heartening, to think this idea might have a small role to play in making the world a better, healthier place – but I can say for sure that it has long since outgrown a simple trial in a small South Pacific country.

It is my wish that business leaders, policymakers, workers' unions and climate and equal pay campaigners will collectively recognise the value of the four-day week movement and put their energy into bringing our work practices into the twenty-first century. This book is written as a simple guide to the rationale and implementation of the four-day week.

I hope it helps.

Andrew Barnes
Auckland, New Zealand
December 2019

CHAPTER ONE

The World of Work As It Is Today

THE WORKING LIFE

Listen to the lyrics of Bruce Springsteen and you will be transported back to an era when work outside the home was masculine and predominantly manual, with a schedule ruled by the factory whistle. In some ways little had changed since the First Industrial Revolution. Throughout the nineteenth century, workers toiled for long hours, often until they dropped – and from an early age. They also worked predominantly in one job, often for one company, the luckiest or the most capable rising through the ranks on the shop floor or in the management office until they retired (or expired). The only sabbatical was a tour of duty in khaki or blue.

It was only as labour organised that the work week shortened. In the 1870s, full-time work generally consisted of 60 to 70 hours per week, or 3,000-plus hours a year. With the strengthening of the labour movement, increasing affluence and technological advances in the decades after World War II, in most developed countries the average working week settled at around 40 hours.[1]

While this gradual downward trend has continued in Germany, where the trade union IG Metall recently won the right to a 28-hour week for 900,000 workers,[2] and France, which famously has a mandated 35-hour week, it has reversed in the United States and the United Kingdom, where hours have risen since the turn of the millennium. Statistics published by the Organisation for Economic Co-operation and Development (OECD) in 2018 place the US near the top of developed countries for hours worked per year – 1,786, nearly 250 hours more than the UK. Germany clocked the lowest annual hours, at 1,363.*[3,4,5]

Meanwhile, work as a social and economic construct is becoming less stable among several demographics, especially school leavers and those over 50. *The New World Order*, a

---

* Average annual hours worked is defined as the total number of hours actually worked per year divided by the average number of people in employment per year. Actual hours worked include regular work hours of full-time, part-time and part-year workers, paid and unpaid overtime, and hours worked in additional jobs, and exclude time not worked because of public holidays, annual paid leave, own illness, injury and temporary disability, maternity leave, parental leave, schooling or training, slack work for technical or economic reasons, strike or labour dispute, bad weather, compensation leave and other reasons. The data covers employees and self-employed workers.

On a per-week basis, work hours rise dramatically when only full-time workers are measured. According to 2011 data from the United Kingdom's Office of National Statistics, the average full-time UK work week runs to 42.7 hours, compared with 41.6 hours across the EU. On this metric, Americans outstrip everyone; a Gallup poll found the work week had been consistently long in the early years of this century, averaging close to 47 hours.

The report that Gallup released on 29 August 2014 showed the average time worked by full-time employees has ticked up to 46.7 hours a week, or nearly a full extra 8-hour day. Just 40 per cent of Americans who work full-time say they clock the standard 40 hours a week. Another 50 per cent say they work more than that.

The work week is even longer for salaried workers (an average of 49 hours), likely because employers don't have to worry about paying them overtime. According to the Gallup poll, half of salaried full-time employees said they work 50 or more hours each week. See https://news.gallup.com/poll/175286/hour-workweek-actually-longer-seven-hours.aspx

2017 report by the Foundation for Young Australians (FYA), identified that one in three Australians under the age of 25 are unemployed or underemployed; 70 per cent of young people will enter the labour market in jobs that will soon be automated or not exist at all; and one-third of jobs created in Australia over the past 25 years have been in temporary work, part-time work or self-employment. While some of these jobs are in developing industries with good prospects, many are less secure, such as work in call or distribution centres linked to online retailers, and these roles will soon be replaced by artificial intelligence, automation and robotics.

A major conclusion of the report is that Australian workers are at risk of losing their minimum wage, insurance and leave entitlements – that is, the basic protections won and entrenched over decades of labour organisation.[6] And in this, they are not alone.

Yet employment uncertainty is not just the province of youth. At the other end of the age spectrum, a report by the San Francisco Federal Reserve based on the largest age-discrimination study ever conducted found that older workers are being excluded even from low-skilled jobs. To test their hypothesis that age discrimination was a broad trend in the US, the researchers created 40,000 fake CVs for 13,000 genuine positions. The outcomes led them to conclude that '[t]here is a distinct pattern of callback rates being highest for the young applicants, lower for the middle-aged applicants, and lowest for the old applicants ... [and] women face worse age discrimination than men', possibly because 'the effects of aging on physical appearance are evaluated more harshly for women than for men'.[7]

This represents a considerable challenge as longer life expectancy, combined with often inadequate retirement savings, forces individuals to keep working long after the traditional age of retirement.

The US topped developed countries for 1,786 hours worked per year, while Germany clocked the lowest at 1,363.

1,786 hours

1,363 hours

Even for those in steady employment, the working life is unrecognisable from just a couple of decades ago. The advent of the internet and smartphone has reformed and redefined our relationship with work. A 2015 poll of white-collar American workers commissioned by Adobe Systems Inc found the respondents spent 6.3 hours a day checking emails, with more than nine in ten checking personal emails at work and nearly as many monitoring business emails outside working hours. Thirty per cent logged in to check emails before even getting out of bed in the morning, and half did so while on holiday.[8]

Arguably, for many people the time we now spend connected to work in the evenings and weekends and while on leave has made obsolete the rule of 'business hours', and replaced it with a state of perma-working reflected in our patterns of internet usage. According to Ofcom, the UK communications services regulator, by 2018 consumers were reporting spending an average of 24 hours a week online, twice as much as a decade ago, with one in five adults spending up to 40 hours a week on the internet. Fifteen per cent of contributors to the Ofcom report said smartphones made them feel they were always at work, 54 per cent admitted smartphone usage interrupted face-to-face conversations with friends and family, and 43 per cent said they spent too much time online.[9]

The intrusion of work into personal time not only disrupts normal family activity and limits the thinking, relaxing and recharging workers were previously able to do in their downtime, but the health ramifications can also be severe. Occupational psychologist Dr Christine Grant told the BBC, 'The negative impacts of this "always-on" culture are that your mind is never resting, you're not giving your body time to recover, so you're always stressed. And the more tired and stressed we get, the more mistakes we make. Physical and mental health can suffer.'[10] It comes as no surprise that stress and mental health issues (often work-related) can be viewed as a modern pandemic.

Today, the quality, length and intensity of the working life is determined by either employment legislation or labour organisation. If the former is eroded, evaded or disregarded, and the latter is a spent force, the worker is on his or her own. Historically, organised labour was a leading determinant of working hours, achieving milestones such as the eight-hour day and the five-day week. And, tellingly, the UK and US, in contrast to the nations of continental Europe, now have relatively disempowered trade union movements.

In Chapter Three we will explore in depth how the gig economy and Agile work practices have emerged as the corporate response to this disempowerment, not mandated by government but grandfathered into the existing employment framework. The advent of the gig economy, operating outside established labour legislation, has allowed companies to exploit so-called personal contracts, often paying workers below the minimum wage and depriving them of standard benefits, while forcing them to work longer hours to cover their living costs.

To add to this, the productivity value of the gig economy is often not reflected in local GDP because multinational owners shunt profits offshore. The services, for example Uber driving or delivery or shared employment spaces, are often provided at a loss in order to grab market share, and are subsidised by capital investment – and there is plenty of capital chasing a limited number of opportunities.

Because the widespread practice of profit exportation is permitted by the exploitation of tax loopholes in many territories, this model often drives traditional service providers out of business and weakens the local contribution of businesses to central and local government revenues. The tax generated by the local activities does not then cover the cost to the country of providing and maintaining the necessary infrastructure to fully support commercial enterprise and sustain a thriving economy.

The early impact of the still-emergent gig economy, sold on the promise of 'work when you want', includes a lengthening of worktimes back towards the first industrial period, evoking the image of huddled masses waiting at the factory gates. It may also preface an extension of the working life itself, not just because of lengthening life expectancy but also owing to the need for wages to top up inadequate savings pots and to meet escalating healthcare costs.

Meanwhile, the move towards agile work practices, disintermediation and automation of basic roles within higher-paying professions is exerting similar pressures on employees. In these arenas, success often hinges on a willingness to focus solely on work to the complete exclusion of family life and outside pursuits. My personal experience in the finance industry, part of which I will explore in the next chapter, is testament to this. Without intervention such as a legislative cap on all participants, those who take time out for leisure or family reasons risk losing opportunities for career advancement to those who sacrifice everything else in the pursuit of glory. There can be particularly severe ramifications for people – women, disproportionately – who step off the career ladder to raise a family or care for aging relatives.

Bruce Springsteen is still a son of working-class New Jersey, but his well-earned privilege now sets him apart from the blue-collar strivers, one of them his own father, who inspired much of his songwriting. He knows, and has conveyed in his music, that work is a defining force of human life, and when it goes wrong – when we do too much of it, or it's back-breaking or soul-crushing, or we can't get it when we need it – the distress can be profound. Extrapolate this across a society, and we find that many of our biggest challenges, from climate change to physical and mental illness to family dysfunction, have elements of their genesis in how we work today.

WORK AND FAMILY

Sheryl Sandberg, the second in command at Facebook, tells a story about her earlier years at Google, when she routinely worked from 7 a.m. to 7 p.m. After her first child was born, she wanted to get home from work while he was still awake. She began leaving the office before 7 p.m., covering her tracks by using tricks like draping a jacket over the back of her chair.

'The subterfuge continued for years' according to a 2017 *Bloomberg* profile of Sandberg. 'Then in 2012, about a month before Facebook's initial public offering, she admitted to a reporter she regularly left work at 5.30. The revelation blared across multiple news outlets. Sandberg worried she would be lectured or fired. Instead, her brazenness was heralded by other female professionals. The women of the legal team at

Yahoo! Inc sent her flowers with a card saying that they, too, were leaving at 5.30.'[11]

This kind of juggling act, necessary even for someone as privileged and relatively insulated, professionally speaking, as Sandberg, is familiar to millions of working people, whether their manoeuvring is in service of caring for children or aging parents or their own mental or physical health. The world of work is now framed by the most diverse family structures in human history. Fertility rates have declined to the point where almost no OECD country has a birth rate above the population replacement rate of two children per woman. As household sizes shrink, the proportion of women in the workforce is higher than ever before; men and women are starting families later in life; and far more women – at least 20 per cent, and up to 40 per cent, of those aged 20 to 49 in European OECD countries – are living in households with no children.[12]

Meanwhile, marriage rates have fallen across the OECD, from 8.1 marriages per 1,000 people in 1970 to 5.0 in 2009, and divorce rates have risen. According to the OECD, '[t]he decline in marriage rates is related to the emergence of more non-traditional family forms, including relationships that involve partners keeping their own place of residency, "weekend-relationships", "living apart together" and civil partnerships. Cohabitation is increasing, and because there are more people cohabiting before marriage, people are older when they marry … In almost all countries across the OECD the younger generation (aged 20–34) is more likely to be cohabiting than the previous generation at the same age.'[13] In all likelihood this reflects two common themes. In many countries the affordability of housing has declined markedly – and where unmarried individuals could previously have afforded to rent or purchase their own home, now two incomes are necessary. Additionally, there is now a widespread view that marriage is no longer a prerequisite for starting a family.

Detailed projections produced by some OECD countries predict changes in household structures in 2025 to 2030, with the number of one-person households predicted to grow in every country for which projections are available, and with estimated increases of up to 73 per cent in Australia, 71 per cent in New Zealand and 60 per cent in the UK.[14] The sole-parent families' share of all households with children is likewise expected to rise, as is the number of couples with no children.[15]

An OECD assessment of the position of women juggling the demands of work and home life is validated by Sandberg's story of leaving her jacket on the chair, and drives home the point that women are often perceived by employers to be a poorer long-term choice:

> Employers are aware that mothers have to make work and family choices. In fact, many employers expect women, regardless of their level of educational attainment, to withdraw (at least temporarily) from the labour force upon marriage and/or childbirth, and are therefore more likely to consider women less committed to their career than men. As a result, employers are less likely to invest in female workers and their career prospects. To some extent this is a vicious circle: as female workers have limited incentives to pursue a career if they perceive the likelihood of moving upwards to be more limited than for men, they are more likely to leave the labour force, thus reinforcing the stereotype. These features apply to most OECD labour markets to some degree.[16]

This negative attitude to an effective balance between work and home life also affects male employees. Seeing how their female colleagues are disadvantaged as they attempt to walk the tightrope between home and work reinforces the view that men who work full-time cannot contribute meaningfully to household and family duties lest it adversely affect their careers. Inevitably, families must recognise the economics of such decisions, and men – who are usually earning more than their female partners – remain working full-time, thus reinforcing the gender pay gap and unequal division of labour at home.

The Sandberg anecdote is revelatory not only for how female workers can feel caught in a no-woman's-land between work and home, but also for what it tells us about how the productivity of a worker is typically measured. How on Earth can a parent who began her work day at 7 a.m. be perceived as committing an act of 'brazenness' by leaving 10.5 hours later to attend to her young child?

Nowhere in the story is it suggested there was any decline in the value of Sandberg's contribution to the business because she shaved a few hours off her work week without permission from HR. Indeed, the fact no one noticed until she made her media confession suggests her productivity was unaffected by a shortened day in the office.

In fairness, Sandberg is probably an outlier. She is one of the highest-achieving women in the history of tech, not an industry known for having a healthy gender balance. But in making a public admission about her work schedule and her fears about her employer's response, Sandberg unwittingly revealed one of the truths about work in the modern digital age: very few employers know how to measure output, so they gauge an employee's value by the number of hours they spend at their desk.

THE PRODUCTIVITY PROBLEM

With fewer people working on assembly lines and more of us working at laptops, a measurement of productivity based upon the number of hours an individual spends at a desk each day is problematic for a host of reasons, not least how it rewards the hyperconnectedness that is proving disruptive to normal social and family activities.

What do we talk about when we talk about productivity? The UK's *Independent* newspaper provides a simple definition:

> It refers to the amount of work produced either per worker or per hour worked. So if a baker produces 10 loaves of bread in an hour's work, his personal bread-making productivity would be 10 loaves per hour. In the context of the entire economy, productivity refers to the amount of GDP (the value of all goods and services) output in a period of time divided by all the hours worked by all the workers in the economy over that same time period.[17]

A complicating factor is that for the many workers who are not responsible for the output of tangible goods for direct sale, their employers have to calculate a) what constitutes worker output; and b) what is an appropriate amount of output, or productivity, per worker per day. The *Economist* article that was the seed of my four-day week cited studies showing British workers were productive for an average of 2.5 hours and Canadian workers for as little as 1.5 hours of a standard eight- or nine-hour work day.

A 2017 UK survey of nearly 2,000 full-time office workers found the average time spent working is 2 hours and 53 minutes each day (a slightly more generous tally than the average cited in the *Economist*), with workers also spending time using social media and reading news websites, making personal calls and texts, talking to co-workers about non-work-related matters, searching for new jobs, taking smoke breaks and preparing food and drinks.[18]

The fact the employers of these workers apparently were not questioning the true level of output from people who were presenting for a full work week of 37 to 40 hours demonstrates that many leaders have little grasp of the productivity – whether actual or theoretical – of those working for them.

When asked, 'Do you consider yourself to be productive throughout the entire working day?', 79 per cent of respondents to the survey said no, and 54 per cent said the distractions listed above made the working day 'more bearable'.[19]

The latter comment is starkly revealing of the effects of work-related stress; those with longer commutes or who work in companies or industries with an expectation of after-hours connectivity might use such extracurricular activities as a form of downtime they cannot otherwise get.

DRIVEN TO DISTRACTION

It is hard to escape the impression that, in swelling numbers across the developed world, workers are being led into a locked room, escape from which can only be triggered by an exceptional event – a windfall like a lottery win or a large inheritance.

In New Zealand, where the house-price-to-income ratio is the third highest globally, after Canada and Ireland,[20] workers in Auckland, the largest and most expensive city in which to buy or rent property, have been fleeing to the provinces in such numbers that schools are now building houses and setting up on-site gyms and childcare services to attract and retain staff.[21]

Certainly the extreme shifts in work and family care patterns have been accompanied by a rise in the cost of living in developed countries, with skyrocketing housing costs to the fore. In the last five years, house prices in major cities have increased by an average of 35 per cent. The president of the Los Angeles

Business Council, Mary Leslie, drove home the effect of house price and corresponding rent rises for the city's workers: 'There will be a breaking point for employees forced to choose between sky-high rents, substandard conditions or long commutes … Housing is not a siloed issue – it has a domino effect far beyond the housing market.'[22]

With housing costs demanding a greater share of workers' take-home pay, a new term has emerged: super-commuter. Across the US, one in thirty-six commuters – nearly 4 million people – meet this definition by spending 90 minutes or more travelling to work each day, mostly in large cities with strong economies.

A key driver, according to one analysis, is that 'new housing is skewed towards the periphery of major cities, rather than urban cores and inner suburbs, forcing many workers to take on longer commutes in exchange for lower home prices.'[23] Another report noted the long shadow of the global financial crisis as a factor in super-commuting; many workers who were affected by the 2008 crisis are reluctant to move.[24]

We have known for some time the debilitating effect of long-term commuting on human health. A 2001 scientific study of more than 400 German commuters, about 90 per cent of whom had trips of more than 45 minutes each way between work and home, found the proportion who reported pain, dizziness, exhaustion and severe sleep deprivation was twice as high as in a control group of non-commuters. The study's leader described the group's psychosomatic condition as 'terrible', and said among the long-distance travellers, '31 per cent of the men and 37 per cent of the women were, from a medical point of view, clearly in need of treatment'.[25]

Other studies, reported the *Scientific American*, 'show that workers who use mass transit suffer from higher infection rates and that car drivers have a greater incidence of joint disease'.[26]

A separate sociological study of long-distance commuters, also in Germany, found almost 60 per cent of respondents had no time for friends or other social interests. Researchers at the University of Zurich's Institute for Empirical Research in Economics surveyed several thousand German households annually from 1985 to 1998 and concluded that 'for every minute longer a worker spends getting to work he will be less satisfied with his life'.[27]

The researchers calculated that between Germans who commuted two hours a day and those with an average commute of 40 minutes, the satisfaction difference was so great it would take a 40 per cent pay rise to compensate for the longer commuters' unhappiness.[28] Furthermore, the longer the commute, the less capacity the worker has to be productive, which can only enhance dissatisfaction.

We need hardly dwell on the damaging effects of mass commuting. Longer rides to work mean more congestion and more of its attendant problems. As a snapshot, in 2011 congestion cost Americans 5.5 billion more hours in travel time and an extra 2.9 billion gallons of fuel, with an overall price tag of $121 billion and 56 billion pounds of carbon dioxide emissions.[29] That is one year in one country, with the effects of congestion measured *on top of* ordinary levels of time, fuel and emissions associated with commuting to work. Extrapolated across the developed world, the real costs are virtually incalculable.

IN SICKNESS AND IN HEALTH

Statistical data and anecdotal evidence are telling us work today, exacerbated by employers' 'always on' expectation and the reluctance or inability of workers to escape the reach of technology, is not only crowding out other activities – it is actually making us sick. As work days are stretched by brutal commutes which deprive people of rest, family time and social time, the workplace itself has been identified as a common cause and intensifier of mental illness. This phenomenon is not exclusive to office workers but affects many in other fields, from the factory floor to classrooms, hospitals and retail stores.

In the UK, work-related stress, anxiety or depression now accounts for 57 per cent of all working days lost to ill health. The Society of Occupational Medicine reports that each year, about 400,000 UK workers report illness which they attribute to work-related stress.[30] Between 2017 and 2018, 15.4 million working days were lost to mental illness connected with work, up from 12.5 million the previous year,[31] racking up a lost output cost to employers and self-employed people of between £33.4 and £43 billion per year, and lost tax or national insurance revenue of between £10.8 and £14.4 billion per year.[32]

These statistics are not isolated but are broadly representative of what we are seeing in much of the world. A *New Zealand Listener* story on workplace depression and anxiety cited a 2016 London School of Economics study of eight countries (including the US, Mexico and Japan) which 'examined the effect of depression on the workplace and the costs associated with both absenteeism and presenteeism (when you are at work but not functioning at your normal level). [The researcher] found it was a considerable issue for all the countries, regardless of their economic development, and collectively it was costing $246 billion a year.'[33]

The causes of mental health problems initiated or exacerbated by work are generally well understood. The World Health Organization identifies work-related risk factors for health as inadequate health and safety policies, poor communication and management practices, low levels of support for employees, inflexible working hours and unclear tasks or organisation objectives, in addition to low control over one's area of work. The organisation notes that responsibility for tasks unsuited to the worker's competencies or a high and unrelenting workload constitute risks, and bullying and psychological harassment are commonly reported causes of work-related stress and consequent psychological and physical problems.[34]

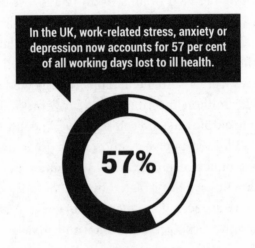

In the UK, work-related stress, anxiety or depression now accounts for 57 per cent of all working days lost to ill health.

57%

A large study of nearly 70,000 mid-life workers by the Black Dog Institute bears this out, finding 'people experiencing higher job demands, lower job control and more job strain were at greater odds of developing mental illness by age 50, regardless of sex or occupation'.[35]

If we were to freeze-frame the world of work as it is today, the picture would be one of enormous economic output at an equally vast human and environmental cost. People are arguably more connected to work – and in many cases overworked – than they have ever been, and weightier workloads are having a crushing effect. Meanwhile, individual productivity is affected by workplace structures which reward presenteeism, not output, and by the macroeconomic influences driving up commuting times and separating families for nearly all of the day's waking hours. Some power, at least, must be in the hands of workers – so what are they trying to do about it?

IN BRIEF

- In the digital age, very few employers know how to measure output, so they gauge an employee's value by the number of hours they spend at their desk.

- Changes in family structures and the extreme shifts in work and family care patterns have been accompanied by a rise in the cost of living in developed countries, with skyrocketing housing costs to the fore. The consequent trend of 'super-commuting' is a factor in epidemic levels of work-related stress and illness.

- As the 'rule' of the 40-hour week is being eroded by rising working hours across much of the world, work as a social and economic construct is becoming less stable among several demographics, especially school leavers and those over 50.

- For many workers subject to employment instability, the gig economy is a lure and a trap, with technology – which enables the gig – becoming the same tool that interferes with rest, relaxation and socialising outside of work. Many employers have an 'always on' expectation and workers are reluctant or unable to escape the reach of technology, contributing to the hyperconnectedness which can trigger or exacerbate stress caused by work.

CHAPTER TWO

The Workers' Response

HUSTLE CULTURE

There is no handbook for how to be a worker in the digital age. The conventions of work as they were understood by the parents and grandparents of millennials have been replaced, or at least displaced. Now, women are nearly as likely as men to undertake paid work outside the home, and with the advent of email, for many office workers and professionals the concept of a defined work day is long gone, outmoded like the flip phone. On-call work, once the province of life-and-death professions like emergency medicine, midwifery and firefighting, has made its way into most white-collar fields, whose practitioners can log on anytime, anywhere.

Workaholics have always roamed among us, but a compulsion to work was previously understood as a choice or, at worst, the product of a specific company's culture, not the manifestation of a larger cultural mandate.

This no longer holds true. The journalist Dan Lyons says

tech culture has made overwork and stress fashionable, and this attitude is spreading to other workplaces. In his book, *Lab Rats: How Silicon Valley Made Work Miserable for the Rest of Us*, he writes that today's workplaces are a mix of a frat house, a kindergarten and a Scientology Assessment Centre. The prevalence of personality tests ('When did we decide that it was okay for our employer to peer into our brain?') is one example of how companies are experimenting on employees with often detrimental effects, he told Radio New Zealand in a March 2019 interview:

> We're in this dawn of this 'Fourth Industrial Revolution' and somehow companies have got the idea that everything they've done for the past 100 years, the way companies have organised themselves, all of it is obsolete, it doesn't make sense any more, the world has changed, and work has to change too.
>
> There is some truth to that, but the bad part is they don't know what does work and, so, companies are engaged in these ongoing experiments essentially using us, human beings, employees, as the lab rats where they try one thing and they try another, and they try to make us 'agile' and 'lean' and 'nimble' and 'adaptable'. There are a zillion of these new theories flying around and companies are adopting one or more of them and it's exhausting for employees to be put through this.[1]

In some cases, workers are buying into it. Lyons points to the self-referencing of Amazon employees as 'Amabots' who strive to fit into a 'performance optimisation algorithm' which measures every facet of their work. He says, 'When you go to work now it feels like you're not using the technology; the technology is using you. The technology is actually what's central to the company and you are just an adjunct to that, you just come in and plug into the machine and unplug at the end of the day and your success depends on how well you can do that, how good of a widget you are. It's very dehumanising.'[2]

The collision of technology and performance is expanding the role of work in our lives, others say. In the *New York Times*, Erin Griffith identifies the 'performative workaholism' of a new work culture dubbed 'hustle culture'. Its exponents include Elon Musk, who says 'nobody ever changed the world on 40 hours a week'. He views an 80-hour week as about right.

Griffith theorises that ceaseless work is filling another void.

Perhaps we've all gotten a little hungry for meaning. Participation in organised religion is falling, especially among American millennials. In San Francisco, where I live, I've noticed that the concept of productivity has taken on an almost spiritual dimension. Techies here have internalized the idea – rooted in the Protestant work ethic – that work is not something you do to get what you want; the work itself is all. Therefore any life hack or company perk that optimises their day, allowing them to fit in even more work, is not just desirable but inherently good.[3]

Some workers who find themselves immersed in the hustle culture will thrive, and perhaps those with a Herculean work ethic, a love of what they do, and few commitments outside work will feel genuinely rewarded. But the billionaire head of Tesla Motors is working up to 100 hours a week by choice. If this is what anyone is having to do just to get by, or because their company or industry culture dictates it, something is terribly wrong.

THE ART OF SELF-MANAGEMENT

Bestseller lists have long been occupied by titles filled with advice on how to better ourselves, and now that creators have figured out how to spread their messages across platforms (see: Marie Kondo's joy-sparking path from books to Netflix), self-improvement can happen anywhere.

Even a reviewer of Cal Newport's bestselling *Deep Work: Rules for Focused Success in a Distracted World* was moved to follow the rules prescribed in the book she was examining, calling her iPhone a 'bad tenant' that should be banished from her life. She reported that by the hundred-page mark she had powered down her laptop, bought an alarm clock to use instead of her phone's alarm, and asked her brother to block her access to Twitter.[4]

The piece is wry and a little tongue-in-cheek, but it perfectly captures the perils of connectivity and the difficulty workers have in detaching from technology, particularly if their work depends wholly or in part on an internet connection. As the reviewer says, 'Many of us couldn't quit email any more than we could quit electricity or running water.'[5]

Googling the phrase 'work hacks' yields about 71,000 results, with advice on how to 'make life at a desk easier' and 'instantly make a day at the office more fun'. The web is replete with tips to improve personal productivity, and that's before you get to the books and podcasts. Similarly, the TED category on work has speakers telling us how to work smarter, work happier, learn the meaning of work, find out why you should treat the tech you use at work like a colleague. If you want, you can enter the 'side-hustle revolution' through a TED portal.[6]

Many workers are grappling with how to use the internet to make their lives better while managing the degree to which it intrudes. A study conducted by Dr Larry Rosen, an expert on the impact of technology and an emeritus professor at

California State University, found those with higher social media usage had more symptoms of psychiatric disorders – and, as we know, a lot of unproductive time in the workplace is accounted for by visits to popular websites, including social platforms.[7]

For some workers, a solution can be found in software programmes that block certain websites or even stop access to the internet for a period of time. The founder of one such programme, called Freedom, says changes in working habits, such as an increase in remote working, mean people need more help to maintain productivity and reduce distractions.[8]

Tim Ferriss's *The 4-Hour Workweek* has sold 1.3 million copies since its publication in 2007, and the popularity of its messages – nine to five is arbitrary; you don't have to live behind a desk until retirement; freedom awaits you – is perennial, even if commentators such as Meagan Day, writing in the *Jacobin*, dismissed the book as 'dozens of pages of self-help and time-management clichés' followed by 'his magic bullet solution: *follow in his footsteps and become a fake expert*'.[9] It is not clear how many people have parlayed Ferriss's advice into emancipation from a desk.

In real life, almost no one is lamenting being desk-bound or that work itself isn't fun enough. Lots of people happen to enjoy their work, but there has never been a cultural expectation that work is the place you go or the thing you do to have a good time.

Yet, as we've seen in Chapter One, workers are getting sicker *because* of work, and many are doing what they feel is necessary to manage it. Anecdotally, workers are increasingly protecting their well-being through what are dubbed 'mental health days'. The case of a web developer in Michigan who requested two sick days to focus on her mental health exemplifies an ideal. In a 2017 tweet, since shared more than 15,500 times, she noted that her boss had not only approved her leave but thanked her for helping to 'cut through the stigma' of mental health.[10]

In a 2018 column on the *Stuff* website, Tony Stevens writes that he felt guilty for taking a mental health day while under extreme stress, and that 'across the world, the cultural response to mental health in the workplace is troubling ... workplaces haven't caught up with the important discussions happening in wider society'. He says workers with mental health needs don't often feel safe telling their boss, and 'many employers do not attribute the same respect to mental safety as they do to physical safety', even as '[t]he World Health Organization warns that mental illness will be the primary cause of disability and absence in the workplace by 2030 if we don't act now'.[11]

There are fixes, Stevens writes, but the will needs to come from both sides; employers should encourage days off to protect and restore mental health, and workers should stop trying to tough it out. Of course, there is only so much workers can do in the face of an intractable or oblivious employer, and bosses cannot act outside the legislative framework. Stevens also recommends a law change to provide a higher minimum entitlement for sick leave days and that mental health be explicitly referenced as a valid reason to use that entitlement.[12] Workers cannot move the dial on their own, and their very status as employees limits their ability to demand or enforce all the entitlements they need.

THE RESISTANCE

We know that revolutionary changes in structures of work – the kind that measurably improve the lives of workers, such as mandated reductions in hours and comprehensive leave entitlements – have historically only come about when labour organisers and workers combined their energies and skill sets.

As long-held standards such as the eight-hour day come under informal but relentless pressure from corporate interests (which we will address in Chapter Three), incremental advances against the shifting rules of work are being made by workers themselves. A landmark case in the United Kingdom addressing the employment status of a plumber exemplifies this employee-led progress.

Gary Smith had worked for Pimlico Plumbers for six years and, not withstanding his 'self-employed' status, contended that he was a 'worker' with corresponding valuable employment rights under the law, such as holiday pay. Pimlico Plumbers, established in 1979, is London's largest independent plumbing company. The company avoided paying PAYE (pay as you earn) and national insurance for its tradespeople by hiring them as 'self-employed contractors' who are responsible for paying their own tax.[13]

In response to an appeal by Pimlico Plumbers, the Supreme Court upheld earlier rulings by the Employment Appeal Tribunal and the Court of Appeal, and took the view that 'the fact that Pimlico exercised tight administrative control over Smith, imposed conditions around how much it paid him and on his clothing and appearance for work, and restricted his ability to carry out similar work for competitors if he moved on from the company, all supported the conclusion that he was a "worker" and not genuinely self-employed'.[14]

As was reported at the time of the June 2018 ruling, this decision in relation to an ostensibly self-employed plumber has implications for all UK organisations operating in the gig economy, where workers are treated as self-employed or independent contractors even when companies may hold sway over when, where and how they work.

Clearly, a groundswell is building in favour of the traditional rights of workers. On the heels of the Pimlico Plumbers case, the United Kingdom Court of Appeal upheld an Employment Appeal Tribunal decision that Uber was wrong to classify its drivers as independent contractors, and basic rights such as minimum wage and holiday pay must be afforded.[15]

With Uber's standard technical defence against such challenges – that it is not an employer but an agent connecting independent drivers with customers – finding a cool reception in the courts, the company is holding fast to its core promise. After the Court of Appeal's decision, a company spokesperson warned that if drivers were classified as workers they would inevitably lose some freedom and flexibility. Uber will appeal to the Supreme Court.

While these cases have set a precedent for workers to use the courts to secure – or restore – conventional labour benefits, there appears to be little appetite at a legislative level to add protections to all contracts. Perhaps policymakers are more comfortable on the sidelines; it is far easier to watch the judiciary address the problem than risk the ire of large corporates by wading in themselves.

Should they choose to act and spare workers the extraordinary costs typically associated with a legal action, there are two obvious legislative remedies. The law could be amended to stipulate either that all contracts have benefits attached, or that certain types of contracts are deemed to be employment contracts. Currently, the UK is the closest in having a category of 'worker' with rights to all employment benefits except redundancy (statutory pay) and unfair dismissal.

Is this the beginning of a new labour movement? Could

the mounting resistance to the independent-contractor model extend to the continued erosion of the rights of workers by companies as a result of the rise of hustle culture and hyperconnectivity? My own experience suggests even the most industrious among us have a breaking point, and once you have snapped, there's no going back.

STRESS AND THE CITY

My breaking point as a worker was accompanied by an epiphany. After ten years at Macquarie Group in Australia, one of the world's pre-eminent investment banks, I had attained the position of Executive Director, one of the senior executive positions in the group, in charge of the retail, private and equity banking operations. By all measures of success in a savage industry, I was a winner. But my marriage had fallen apart, and the prevailing workplace culture had become toxic with interpersonal intimidation and extraordinary competitive ruthlessness. The job was nothing more than an endurance test, and I hated my life.

This was all to be expected, of course. My formative years in the finance industry prior to Macquarie were in the City of London in the 1980s, where work was defined by a punishing schedule. Apparently, in order to compete with our American investment banking rivals, we had to get into the office before the Tokyo stock market closed at 7.30 a.m. and leave after New York had opened 12 hours later. With my commute and the vagaries of British Rail, this meant getting up just after 5 a.m. and arriving home after 10 p.m.

This pattern held until one night in the office, when my boss, Harry, broke down in front of me. I had been taught from almost my first day that to leave work before my manager was career suicide, even though he lived much closer to the office than me and obeying the rule meant forgoing a lot of much-needed rest. When I witnessed Harry succumbing to the inhuman strain of our industry's culture, I understood for the first time that he was under the same pressure I was. He drove his underlings so hard because he needed his team to perform to a standard that impressed his superiors.

Harry's public mental collapse didn't cause a ripple in upper management. The diagnosis of post-traumatic stress had not yet been identified, and any discussion about mental health in the workplace was still years away. To Harry's credit, he reacted to his own moment of crisis by changing what he could. I still had to get up before dawn to attend company-mandated early meetings, but now I only had to work 10- to 12-hour days and could catch an earlier train home. Harry was the first person I worked with to recognise that the productivity equation was not calculated on the number of hours worked, and his team could be just as productive in a shorter work day. Sadly, Harry's mental collapse owing to work-induced stress would not be the last I would witness in my City career.

Others found ways to let off steam that made the capitalist hysteria of the Big Bang era look like a black comedy. Two university friends of mine were working at a Japanese bank in London where being the last person to leave the office was a badge of honour. My friends decided to use the very late nights as a weapon to break their bosses, and would tag-team all evening – taking turns to pop out and return to the office – the objective being to outlast their Japanese team leader while each getting the respite they needed and artfully avoiding any penalty.

In the end, the management caved. Their 'solution' was to install a bedroom in the office so senior executives could rest and none of that group would lose face. The staff had no right to question the punishing schedule the institution demanded of them; instead a solution was fabricated so managers themselves could survive the same regime they were inflicting on employees.

Extreme though this may have been, I grew accustomed to the culture of the City and was not surprised when I moved to Australia and my London-based boss would frequently call me at 2 a.m. It was a convenient business hour for him, and no concession was ever made for the difference in time zones.

As my twenties passed in a blur of endless work, my personal life took a back seat. Actually, it wasn't even in the car, but running along behind, barely visible through a cloud of dust. The solution many of my colleagues found was to date those they worked with – otherwise you would never see each other. At a middle-of-the-night closing documentation session in Australia, a young lawyer told me she treated these long, intense meetings like speed-dating events – it was her best chance of meeting someone. I knew what she meant; when I finally got married, it was to a co-worker.

For a long time, my philosophy was a product of this culture. Overworking and treating people like racehorses – to be whipped, to do your bidding, to make money – are alarmingly easy habits to replicate when they are all you know.

Then came the moment of crisis and the epiphany. I was walking across Rushcutter's Bay Park in Sydney and contemplating a line from Nick Hornby's novel *Fever Pitch*: 'Is life shit because Arsenal are shit, or the other way round?' Or rather, was my life in Sydney shit because of my work, or was my work shit because my life was?

You know you have hit bottom when you are pondering that as a serious philosophical question. In that moment, I admitted to myself that I despised the person I had become. I had to get out. And I made a pact with myself that in every business I worked in from then on, I would do things differently. In the last 18 years of my working life, it has been surprisingly easy to keep this promise. In any important workplace scenario where my decision is needed, I silently ask, *What would Macquarie have done?* Then I do precisely the opposite.

THE NEW OPIATE

We cannot speak honestly about today's workers without addressing the intersection of work and consumerism, or analysing how the time poverty caused by demanding jobs and lengthening commutes is making convenience a self-perpetuating force and the first choice in consumer decisions. The ugly truth is that workers, as consumers, are feeding the expansion of a new economic model that is in turn steadily undermining the worker protections that have been won, piece by painstaking piece, since the First Industrial Revolution.

When Karl Marx derided religion as 'the opium of the people', Uber Eats was still 170-odd years from its genesis. Now we are smartphone junkies – we talk of social media holidays and deliberate disconnection as triumphs of the will. Technology is immediacy, and to wait for anything feels like a regression to some uncomfortable, devolved state. Observe people in a queue, peering down at their handheld screens. We can no longer stand quietly with our own thoughts, but must be constantly stimulated, searching, surfing.

In the developed world at least, religion has lost its narcotic lure. The twenty-first-century opiate of choice is convenience, and it feeds, or perhaps conceals, a profound cognitive dissonance. We fret about climate change while using an e-scooter to travel a distance we are capable of walking because it is cheap, convenient and has the 'cool' factor absent in the buses and bicycles which produce a much lower per-user carbon footprint.

When we make this choice, we barely consider the environmental impact of the scooter's manufacture, recharging and
cost of collection. It scores negatively on every metric except
the buzz we get from zipping two kilometres (or less) past
rush-hour traffic to meet a friend for an after-work drink – and
that is all the justification we need.

What we call ride-sharing taps into the same part of the
psyche, which is thrilled by innovation and price reduction.
The taxi industry did not historically attract much attention
or organised capital, but the model worked well enough for
owners, and the established companies were almost comically
complacent in failing to innovate and evade the tech-based
tsunami that was headed their way for years.

The original concept of ride-sharing, now all but forgotten, applied an Airbnb structure to private vehicles: we
would evolve to an urban-sophisticate model of syndicate car
ownership, or be driven taxi-style in a kind of carpool with
strangers. The popular theory had this leading to fewer cars,
more efficiency and reduced personal transport costs. What
has emerged instead is a large fleet of cars delivering precisely
the opposite of the 'green' footprint that was initially contem-
plated – and provided by drivers regularly earning below the
minimum wage.

As with e-scooters, when presented with more sustainable
options such as walking, cycling or public transport, we tend
to choose Uber. Why? Rationally, when presented with a set
of choices in the context of an environmental or ethical debate,
we know what is right and responsible, and make informed
decisions. In practice, however, convenience usually trumps
all, and it's easy to believe the PR campaigns of well-organised
(and well-funded) disrupters which are seen as 'cool'.

If we are increasingly leaning towards the physically lazier
choice, and e-motoring when we could be deriving the benefits

of walking, we are also applying less intellectual rigour to how we live. Our everyday choices are likely to be influenced by online recommendations crafted by algorithms and easily bought and sold, along with our internet search history, e-commerce habits and other factors we scarcely understand, such that independent thought and research are now super-fluous to the purchasing process. We know all this, yet when the 'best' – almost always the most convenient – option is presented as a solution, we choose it, no effort required. Convenience trumps everything else.

Consequently, we do not ask how a garment can be so cheap, how Uber or Lyft can provide transportation for a fraction of the cost of a traditional taxi, or how an overnight delivery service can be provided when it clearly doesn't cover the cost of service – certainly not at minimum wage rates.

A direct line has been drawn from Karl Marx to Mark Zuckerberg, and we find ourselves kneeling at the altar of convenience, holding our shiny mobile devices in place of dusty hymn books, basking in the full power of technology. The gig economy is the apparently limitless manifestation of consumer demand, abetted by the unprecedented power of the digital revolution. It is also a product of unprecedented corporate might.

If someone is paying the price and it's not the corporation or the consumer, it has to be the gig worker – either by sacrificing income or increasing working hours, or both.

Brief history of a parcel

If convenience is an altar, let us examine what is being sacri-ficed upon it. A consumer – call him Joe – orders a Christmas gift, a commonplace household item, through a popular global website headquartered in another country. In tracking the passage of Joe's parcel we can evaluate the real price of convenience.

- The item is available from a number of e-vendors, but the price and terms of delivery are most favourable at one of the world's largest online retailers, which runs a sophisticated online platform supported by warehouses throughout the United States. Joe lives in New Zealand and the retailer promises fast shipping in time for Christmas morning. His choice of vendor is the most efficient in delivery time and personal expense.

- In the lead-up to peak season, the e-retailer Joe is buying from has amassed a temporary army of gig workers responsible for packing and labelling orders ready for shipping. These workers have no benefits or entitlements, and if they are deemed too slow or ineffective by a supervisor, they will not be rostered for another shift. The assigned worker fulfils Joe's order at the warehouse and hands the parcel off for shipping.

- On the US mainland, a truck driver working on an independent (gig) contract transports the parcel to the nearest port for air freighting. The environmental impact of the truck, from road wear (up to tens of thousands of times more than a standard car, depending on size and weight) to diesel pollution and congestion, is not factored into the cost of Joe's item; part of the mass appeal of this e-retailer is that it does not impose shipping or other costs to offset climate effects. The drivers' lack of leverage with large employers means their hours and rates of pay can continually be squeezed, and as independent contractors, none of the normal employment protections apply. As a category, they are on the verge of redundancy due to continued innovation and development of drones and driverless vehicles.

- The parcel is processed at Los Angeles International Airport, packed in a secure shipping container and loaded into the cargo hold bound for Auckland. The airport workers who handle Joe's parcel in both airports are unionised and have comprehensive legal entitlements and protections. These include overtime allowances to compensate them for longer and additional shifts during high-volume peak periods.

- Joe's parcel wings across the Pacific on a direct flight of 6,500 miles, or around 10,500 kilometres. The logistics provider calculates the carbon footprint of the parcel, based on its payweight (2 kilograms and 0.2 cubic metres), as 230.68 kilograms CO_2.[16] As in the road freight stage of the parcel's journey, the environmental cost of its transportation by air is not met, even fractionally, by Joe or the retailer; speed was a key selling point for Joe, and delivery has been promised within five working days of the date of order.

- After screening and processing at Auckland International Airport by cargo handlers and customs agents on permanent employment contracts offering entitlements such as employer superannuation contributions (mandated by New Zealand law) and the prime benefit of subsidised health insurance, the parcel is handed over to a gig courier for urgent delivery.

- For the driver, delivery times are a key component of his contract. Unexpected congestion in the city means he must work longer hours to ensure all deliveries are made within the paid-for timeframe. If he fails to meet his deadlines, he's out of a job, and there are plenty of workers within the young, low-skilled migrant population who can fill his seat.

- The parcel arrives at Joe's home on time and in perfect condition.

The true cost of Joe's parcel is almost impossible to calculate, but in the short term it includes substantial carbon emissions in two countries and international airspace, and contributes to compromised conditions for numerous workers.

Longer term, the e-retailer's use of its considerable political and economic might enables it to secure a negligible tax obligation outside its primary jurisdiction and undercut its competition in various international markets. This contributes to less investment in labour and underfunding of key infrastructure along key routes on which, ironically, parcel deliveries like Joe's depend. In a globe-spanning contest between convenience and ethics, the easy choice is the clear winner. Meanwhile, the unseen costs of rapid consumption quietly mount.

IN BRIEF

- As the tech industry has become a dominant economic, social and cultural force, overwork and stress have become fashionable and given rise to a new work culture known as 'hustle culture'.

- When punishing work schedules become the norm, workers at every level pay the price with their physical and mental health.

- Workers are starting to push back against erosion of their traditional rights and protections using the courts in various jurisdictions, but legislative action is rare.

- Cheap consumer goods and ultra-convenient services are enormously appealing to buyers and users, but the cost savings usually come at the expense of the gig worker, who is likely to be working longer hours at less than minimum wage to make the numbers add up for the corporation as the gig owner.

CHAPTER THREE

The Corporate Response

THE ORIGINS OF THE GIG

For many business leaders, their first response to the promise made by the four-day week – that of flexibility in work with no compromise to productivity or corporate profitability – is that it already exists: we have the gig economy. Indeed, for the corporation the 'gig' has advantages in that it is relatively simple to implement and has little of the apparent complexity of the four-day week.

It should come as no surprise that 'gig' has evolved in the United States, with its – by international standards – less than generous worker benefits and protections and its high cost of healthcare provision. In such circumstances the transfer of obligations from the corporation to the worker is clearly attractive.

The gig worker receives little beyond income and flexible hours – they get none of the benefits that have become standard in most of the developed world. The individual sacrifices made by these workers may seem small, but added together, whole economies will become imperilled by a generation of gig workers with nothing to fall back on, often working for global gig owners who pay minimal tax in most of the territories in which they operate. When these workers get old or sick or burn out, who will be expected to support them?

Contrast the gig model with that of the four-day week, a flexibility model which retains worker protections and continues to invest, depending on the size of the company, in local, regional and national economies. All the benefits of the gig are provided with none of the downsides.

But in analysing the origins of the gig against the backdrop of historical economic growth, its allure is hardly surprising. To understand how the principles of the gig stand in opposition to those of the four-day week, we have to go back to its origins and examine the many reasons why it is corrosive to the rights and well-being of workers and the vigour of economies.

Historically, worker advancements have been made incrementally, as the forces of labour organisation have resisted and – here and there – overwhelmed the might of corporate institutions. Today, in the midst of the Fourth Industrial Revolution, characterised by the World Economic Forum as a fusion of technologies that is disrupting almost every industry in every country,[1] the power indubitably lies with the corporation. More specifically, the corporation whose products or services are delivered via a digital platform, giving it the capacity to measure and mediate every interaction, and often to avoid potentially restrictive national legislation given its digital – as opposed to more tangible – presence in multiple countries.

Against the corporate colossus, the worker is reduced to a tool, subject to algorithm and evaluation far beyond what could have been conceived in the early internet age. Not just individuals but entire workforces are now vulnerable to

constructive dismissal. Where the gig economy sits on the con-
tinuum of the Fourth Industrial Revolution – is it an instigator
or a consequence? – is a question for economic historians, but
it is a proudly corporate creation, spreading outward from its
birthplace in the West Coast tech hubs of the United States and
emboldened by free trade, consumer demand and the benign
neglect of governments.

As the venture capitalist Nick Hanauer has noted, revolu-
tions come gradually, and then suddenly.[2] The gig economy
can be viewed as a revolution within a revolution, with its
functions becoming a feature of our lives before we fully
understood what it was. Before the late 2000s, the word 'gig'
had only one meaning: it denoted a performance of some
kind, usually musical.[3] The usage changed suddenly when the
global financial crisis took hold, and the phrase 'gig economy'
emerged to describe how Americans were staving off des-
titution by working multiple jobs at once, typically without
contracts or benefits.

In 2015, the *Financial Times* formalised 'gig economy' as a
noun and noted that where it had once been 1920s jazz club
musicians who toiled without healthcare, pensions, paid
holidays or other benefits, the new century's technology made
it possible for anyone with a car or spare bedroom to be a
gig-economy worker, thanks to the seductively simple user
interfaces of ride-sharing apps and platforms such as Airbnb.[4]*

A series of lawsuits against two of the biggest tech companies to rely on gig-economy labour, Uber and Lyft, led
to reviews of what gig work offers those who do it. Alana
Semuels reported in the *Atlantic* that a 2018 California
Supreme Court ruling went to the heart of the gig economy's

---

* Gig economy definition: 'The freelance economy, in which workers support themselves with a variety of part-time jobs that do not provide traditional
benefits such as healthcare.'

contradiction: employers say workers love the flexibility of independent contracting, which lets them set their own hours, while labour advocates warn that companies are dodging their responsibilities and pushing what were once business costs back to workers, who no longer receive once-standard worker protections and benefits.*

A hallmark of the gig economy is a lack of reliable quantitative data capturing the opinions and desires of workers. In the California setting Semuels describes, there are plenty of people declaring what is best for workers, but very little is heard from the workers themselves. Unlike the four-day week model, which is best led by employees, no one, it seems, is asking drivers for Lyft or Instacart or Postmates whether they would rather be independent contractors or employees.[5] The decision has already been made for them.

DEVIL'S BARGAIN

A successful professional woman dies suddenly in an accident and is met at the Pearly Gates by St Peter, who is frank

---

* The *Atlantic* article stated: 'Gig-economy companies lobbied the state to override the [Supreme Court] ruling, claiming that workers would lose their jobs, while labour advocates predicted that it would ensure that fewer people would have to rely on the state safety net. As usual, many of the people engaged in the debate about what's best for workers were not the workers themselves.

'But while the policy debate rages on, a real-world experiment has been testing what, exactly, *would* happen if companies had to switch a large swath of their workers from independent contractors to employees. As of January 1 of this year, cannabis-delivery workers are mandated by state law to be classified as employees. These rules, adopted after Californians voted to legalise marijuana in 2016, are a way for law enforcement to ensure that dispensaries take responsibility for their product, and that it is being handled by trained employees. Since they were enacted, dispensaries around California have started the process of switching delivery drivers, and in some cases other workers as well, from independent contractors to employees. Their experience highlights, more than any hypothetical debate, how there is no one easy answer for how to best structure the gig economy.'

about his conundrum: 'People in your line of work don't usually make it up here, so my orders are to let you have a day in Hell and a day in Heaven. Then it's up to you where you want to spend eternity.'

The woman has two of the best days she could have imagined in life or in death. Upon arriving in Hell she is met by old and new friends, with whom she enjoys a round of golf at a beautiful country club, followed by a sumptuous dinner and dancing. She meets the Devil and finds him utterly charming. Everyone is happy and chatty and shakes her hand as she departs.

Her day in Heaven is spent relaxing on clouds, playing the harp and singing. It's pure bliss. St Peter returns. 'It's time to choose,' he says.

The woman has her answer ready. 'I'd never have thought I'd say this, but Hell was so much fun. I had a great time, and the people were so nice. That's where I want to spend eternity.'

St Peter grants her wish. But this time when the doors to Hell open, a vast grey nothingness stretches out before her. All the people are miserable, and there's no country club or dancing to be seen. The Devil is there, and she turns to him and wails, 'What happened?! I chose Hell because it was a party!'

The Devil shrugs and smiles. 'Yesterday we were recruiting you. Today you're staff.'

This joke, versions of which have been circulating for years, could have been written about the gig economy's promise of a workers' paradise: work when you want, be your own boss, flexibility is king. With seductive lines like these, it's no surprise the gig economy has – to borrow old web-parlance – gone viral. In this new work construct, people in Auckland

and Austin and Amman are tapping into the same ride-sharing apps to buy or sell a simple gig-based service.

Freedom and flexibility are the gifts of the gig, but in exchange some elements intrinsic to how work has formed and reformed in the industrial era have all but vanished. In the gig economy, work is free of all established benefits, from a mandated minimum wage to holiday pay and sick pay. Paid parental leave, bereavement leave, superannuation contributions from the employer – all gone. In fact, there is no employer, because there is no 'job' in the traditional sense. Never has the phrase 'working to live' been more apt.

It did not happen by accident. Susan Fowler is a former software engineer for Uber whose February 2017 blog post exposed the company's *Game of Thrones*-style management culture, problematic treatment of female employees and extensive pattern of internal misconduct. She subsequently wrote an unvarnished account for *Vanity Fair* ('What Have We Done?' Silicon Valley Engineers Fear they have Created a Monster) pinpointing the vulnerability of workers and the cynicism of companies that are blithely dismantling employment protections while touting the appeal of the gig economy in why-would-you-not catchphrases: 'Set your own schedule' (Uber); 'Be your own boss' (Lyft).

Fowler reports overhearing two colleagues discussing how to manipulate bonuses in order to 'trick' drivers into working longer hours.[6] Tech companies are thrilled by algorithms, because they work; however, they are also transparent, and after a 2018 study by the New York Taxi and Limousine Commission found that 85 per cent of New York City's gig-economy drivers were earning less than the city's $15-an-hour minimum wage, the commission announced that from mid-January 2019, Uber, Lyft, Via and Gett/Juno would be required to pay on-demand drivers a minimum of $17.22 an hour after expenses.

In the commission's calculation, this figure is equivalent to the minimum wage plus the extra costs incurred by freelancers in taxes and to compensate for contractors not receiving paid time off. The commission says the change will result in an average rise of nearly $10,000 a year in earnings for 96 per cent of the 80,000 drivers who drive regularly for ride-sharing firms in the city.[7]

Fowler hit the nail on the head when she wrote of the gig's nascent allure, 'The gig-economy ecosystem was supposed to represent the promised land, striking a harmonious egalitarian balance between supply and demand: consumers could off-load the drudgery of commuting or grocery shopping, while workers were set free from the Man.'

The gig economy proves definitively that when something seems too good to be true, it probably is. Workers desire and value flexibility, but the malign truth about the brave new world of the gig is that, almost overnight, we collectively Doctor Frankensteined ourselves into a bold economic model whose ramifications we scarcely understood. Or worse – as the headline of Fowler's *Vanity Fair* article suggests – we allowed a handful of tech whizzes in a tiny corner of the globe to unleash the monster upon us.

A MILLENNIAL DREAM – OR A LONG CON?

This is the crux of the gig economy's promise: it gives the people what they want. It is often couched in the language of benefiting the worker, with the company accommodating a gig structure because the millennial generation, raised with the internet in their palms, want flexibility above all – and the gig is the response.

I contend that this promise is empty. It's a long con.

Certainly, people desire control over their work schedules. Work-life balance is not a myth and a worker who is permitted to juggle their hours to pick the kids up from school regularly is likely to be more loyal and committed to their work. (Later we will return to this phenomenon, known as social exchange theory.)

However, wanting flexibility doesn't mean wanting to work four or five jobs at once. Few people, if any, want that. The fundamental approach of humans to work hasn't changed since time immemorial; we want money in our pockets and a fulfilling job. We don't want to just be getting by.

As discussed in Chapter One, data from the Foundation for Young Australians (FYA) is indicative of the employment crisis facing millennials across the developed world, with rife underemployment, whole sectors facing automation and a trend towards less stable, more short-term work. With these shifts, standard protections such as the minimum wage and leave entitlements start to slide into obsolescence.

Consider what this means: less than a decade into the advent of the gig economy, the career trajectory of people coming into the Australian workforce – a sizeable cohort in a country that has enjoyed decades of healthy growth – has changed radically from that of the preceding generation.

The findings of the FYA are sobering. The percentage of young people underemployed or in multiple jobs is now so sizeable that even if this trend began to change, through policy implementation or other measures, we can expect a significant proportion of the working population to remain caught in the gig trap for, possibly, some years yet.

The picture is the same in other developed countries. A University of Auckland analysis of a 20-year French study of 10,000 school leavers and university graduates found, in the words of Professor Elizabeth George, 'that if you started off in

one of these relative[ly] non-standard type of work arrangements, like temporary [work] or contracts ... the likelihood of
you changing that was low. You were stuck. And that's really,
really, a bit scary.'[8] One explanation, she says, is that companies using temporary workers have no incentive to invest in
them, and without new skills they cannot advance.

At the same time, agents of the gig economy are applying
the media distortion field to emphasise the benefits and dis-
guise the downsides. A BBC.com advertorial promoting the
services of the accounting industry is peppered with shots of
well-dressed 'independent contractors' in polished-looking,
professional shared workspaces – not a driver or warehouse
packer in sight.[9]

What's more, the gig economy may be harmful to those it
purports to benefit most – the corporations. A recent study by
the University of South Carolina, reported by the *Economist*,
found that keeping shifts consistent and allowing employees
to swap shifts via a mobile app boosted sales at a Gap store
by 7 per cent. The availability of jobs means that if people are
scheduled 'like widgets in a factory', with no flexibility, it can
lead to higher worker turnover, absenteeism and poor service,
thus hurting revenue – and workers can simply 'walk across
the street to another retailer' who provides better conditions.[10]

Ironically, even employees in the privileged epicentre of
tech – people like the engineers Fowler describes, whose jobs
come with high compensation and broad protections – typically
do not last long with one employer. As Emily Chang reports in
her book *Brotopia: Breaking Up the Boys' Club of Silicon Valley*, the
job search company Indeed found software engineers in San
Francisco have the shortest job tenure (just over two years) of
people in the same profession in any metropolitan area, because
of individual ambition and enormous industry opportunity:
'Jobs are "gigs", and short stints are common.'[11]

THE UNDOING OF WORKERS' RIGHTS

Susan Fowler suggests that the rise of a vulnerable class of gig workers is more by design than accident, as 'a spate of lawsuits has highlighted an alarming by-product of the gig economy – a class of workers who aren't protected by labour laws, or eligible for benefits provided to the rest of the nation's workforce'.[12]

Strikes are an established tool of leverage for workers within a conventional, organised employment structure. To unaffected observers, they sometimes resemble Hollywood blockbusters for high stakes and higher blood pressure, such as during the lead-up to Christmas 2018, when representatives of Air New Zealand and airline engineers and logistics workers held tense negotiations over pay and conditions under threat of a three-day strike, which would have caused chaotic disruption to holiday travel for tens of thousands of people and the worse possible PR for the airline. This is a well-trodden path across the developed world – as I write this, workers at Heathrow, the UK's busiest airport, have announced strike action during the peak August holiday season.

In the Air New Zealand case, the crisis was defused by mediation, and the better-off workers presumably enjoyed Christmas Day with a greater-than-usual feeling of goodwill towards humankind. But in a gig economy there are no strikes, no negotiations and no improvements to worker conditions because the employer has no incentive or legal obligation and the worker has no leverage.

In many developed countries, labour organisers and workers' collectives have fought hard for decades to steadily advance and entrench workers' rights in legislation. It seems unwise, to put it mildly, to let this progress go up in smoke for the convenience of an Uber Eats delivery.

The ramifications of the gig economy go far beyond the erosion of workers' rights, however. For many workers, ongoing
professional development is core to their career advancement, but as Professor George identified, in a gig economy
the employer has neither an obligation nor any incentive to
educate or develop their workforce.

Think about it – the biggest companies driving the gig
economy are those which have disintermediated industries
down to an almost assembly-line division of labour. Amazon
wants its worker to deliver a parcel; does it need to invest in
developing that worker's skills? No, because the brief is very
limited. And soon enough, the worker will be replaced with
a drone and even that limited gig will dry up. Uber has its
drivers out in force and is gathering rich data which it will
ultimately use to run driverless cars: 'Your work here is done.
Thanks for playing.'

It is a sobering picture, but I would be remiss not to address
the argument many are making as to the upside of the gig
economy. True, it promises flexibility and self-control of work
that more and more people – from millennials entering the
workforce, to busy workers in midlife, to superannuitants still
in employment – are said to want. The daily grind is undoubt-
edly more tolerable when it does not involve a traffic-clogged
commute to work standard weekday hours. Flexibility has
tremendous appeal to workers for good reason; we all want a
greater sense of control in our days, and to be valued for our
productivity rather than the number of hours we log 'at work'.

But does the gig deliver true flexibility? As we know, lon-
gevity and permanence are becoming foreign concepts even
in well-compensated strata. However, long hours are not, at
least in many realms of American industry. This is because – in
my observation, at least – what is sold as flexibility is actually perma-availability. Gig workers, in making themselves

available to work certain hours, are subject to the gig owner deciding if they get work.

That decision is not driven only by price; the algorithm can also determine that those workers who make themselves most available are at the top of the gig tree. In other words, to be confident of securing steady gig work, the worker has to be on call as much as possible, and those with the most on-call hours win the gigs. This undermines entirely the ostensible primary benefit of gigging.

My other objection to the gig economy is that in its current structure, the risk is borne by the worker while the reward goes straight to the gig owner. Gig workers are on their own, with no benefits. So when they work themselves to the point of burnout, or fall ill, or get old, and they have no savings to draw on because their various low-paid gigs have only just covered their high cost of living, and the gig owner has wrung out their value with no obligation to help them later – who picks up the tab?

We all do. Unless we are willing to see our fellow citizens literally fall by the wayside, we are going to have to use the tax base to cover vastly increased costs in healthcare, entitlements such as superannuation, and other benefits. Any economist would tell you the maths is simple – if more spending is needed in some areas, governments raise funds by cutting services, selling assets, borrowing on the international market or expanding the tax platform.

But why should we tolerate the gig and the long-term economic burden – even peril – it poses when there is a viable model of work which connects workers and companies to protections, legislation and responsibilities? The four-day week provides flexibility while offering employees at least a living wage, and workers and companies are taxed proportionately. It is not about cutting economic corners or enriching a few plutocrats at the expense of many ordinary citizens who only ask for a decent quality of life and the opportunity to provide for their families and save for a future beyond work.

THE PITCHFORKS ARE COMING

If the most logical solution to the problems of the gig economy is legislative – as opposed to waiting and hoping for the big gig companies to spontaneously self-regulate (the business equivalent to turkeys voting for Christmas or Thanksgiving) – the way in is likely through a review of taxation. We are seeing nascent political attempts to deal with the taxation imbalance at a corporate level, though not at the level of workers' rights.

As the *New York Times* reported in December 2018, after prolonged criticism of its practice of manufacturing offshore and stashing profits in foreign territories to avoid tax payments in the United States, Apple took advantage of the new Trump-era tax code to repatriate $252 billion previously held outside the US, and announced a five-year, $30 billion-plus investment and large-scale domestic job creation programme, including a new campus.[13]

Elsewhere, there are semi-serious efforts to combat the tech-tax dodge. In 2018, the United Kingdom's then Chancellor of the Exchequer Philip Hammond announced a digital services tax, applicable from 2020, targeting revenue generated in the UK by the largest and wealthiest internet businesses. These companies have been in the gunsights for years over low tax payments – a government investigation found that Google paid $16 million in UK corporate tax on $18 billion of revenue from 2006 to 2011 – and this might not change under the new rules, which will ask companies to 'self-assess' how much tax they owe.[14]

At the same time, *Bloomberg* reported, the European Union is debating a 3 per cent version of the same tax. Some members are objecting on the grounds that the cost of tax collection would be higher than the revenue it would generate. The move by French lawmakers to tax Facebook, Google and other US tech companies 'plac[ed] France squarely in the cross hairs of President Trump's escalating trade wars', according to a July 2019 *New York Times* report.[15]

The need for individual governments to impose the same rules on multinational tech companies as they do on locally domiciled SMEs and corporates is urgent, if history is our guide. Consider the lesson of eighteenth-century France, with its three classes of society: the nobility, the clergy, and the remaining 97 per cent of the population. The estates of the first two classes paid little to no tax, while everyone else was taxed and charged other dues. The ultimate result? A bloody revolution with lasting consequences for the Old and New Worlds.

The aforementioned Nick Hanauer, who made his enormous wealth partly through an early investment in Amazon and who now lobbies for a higher minimum wage and other benefits for workers, warned on the Politico website that 'pitchforks are coming ... for us plutocrats' if the super-rich do not address rising inequality. In an open letter addressed to 'My Fellow Zillionaires', Hanauer noted that while 'people like you and me are thriving beyond the dreams of any plutocrats in history', the rest of the country was not.

The problem he identified wasn't just inequality, which in his view was intrinsic to any high-functioning capitalist economy. The real problem was that the US was rapidly becoming a feudal society, with the top 1 per cent controlling about 20 per cent of US national income (up from 8 per cent in 1980), and the bottom 50 per cent just 12 per cent of national income.

The analogy Hanauer drew was that of late eighteenth-century France, before the revolution, when society was divided between the ultra-wealthy and the poor, with no middle class. Unless something was done to fix these glaring inequities in the economy, which he viewed as unsustainable by society, Hanauer was clear as to the ultimate outcome: '[T]here is no example in human history where wealth accumulated like this and the pitchforks didn't eventually come out. You show me a highly unequal society, and I will show you a police state. Or an uprising. There are no counter-examples. None. It's not if, it's when.'[16]

One could argue the gig economy is a new form of feudalism, with a handful of rulers (CEOs, founders and entrepreneurs, investors and shareholders) becoming ever richer on the striving, unprotected backs of the masses. Hanauer himself says the US is becoming a less capitalist and more feudal society. The gig is far from the only reason for the widening global wealth chasm, but it can hardly help redress the imbalance: as of 2018, the 26 richest people in the world had the same net worth as the poorest half of the world's population – around 3.8 billion people – and the global population of millionaires (some 42 million people, 'the 1 per cent' in general terms) controlled 44.8 per cent of the world's wealth.[17]

Apropos of Amazon founder Jeff Bezos, whose net worth increased by $24 billion in 2018 alone, the richest person in the world is now *so rich* that even when he paid $38 billion in his divorce settlement in 2019, he did not lose the top spot. (To place this in context, the previous largest divorce settlement in history was $2.5 billion.)[18]

For the record, Amazon exploits the principles of the gig more expansively and expertly than perhaps any other company, and is currently one of only two American businesses to have a market capitalisation exceeding $1 trillion. The

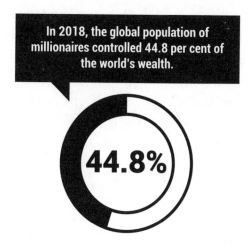

In 2018, the global population of millionaires controlled 44.8 per cent of the world's wealth.

44.8%

other is Apple, whose products are used by countless gig workers.

It may be that the gig economy is symptomatic of a larger amorality arising from the collision of traditional corporate America with the digital age. In *Brotopia*, Emily Chang writes of the retardant effect of Silicon Valley 'bro culture' on the career opportunities and progression of women in tech. She quotes a female entrepreneur jaded by the pervasive imbalance of power between men and women in the industry: 'There is a huge morality issue in Silicon Valley and at the very core, it's people with money thinking they can get away with every-thing. A lot of these guys got lucky, became billionaires on paper, and so they feel they are kings of the universe.'[19]

These observations echo Susan Fowler's remarks on the culture of Uber, and if these attitudes are widely held, it is no wonder workaday people who rely on the gig to make ends meet are becoming a forgotten cohort.

I did not conceive of the four-day week, and I do not now advocate for productivity-focused flexibility in work because I am afraid of pitchforks, but I believe Hanauer's warning is well founded. A society where a handful of people are comparing super-yachts while millions more are unable to reach the relatively modest marks of personal wealth held by their parents and grandparents, such as owning a home, will inevitably break down.

The gig economy, in its current form, is fiscally corrosive and destabilising to society. The good news is that replacing it will take only some shared political and corporate will, with no one having to carry the can on their own. The four-day week offers a clear way forward.

AGILE: HANDLE WITH CARE

Looking back on my 40-year journey from the Royal Navy to Perpetual Guardian, I can identify a consistent pattern in my work. As I see it now, I have repeatedly been drawn to corporate change management roles that presaged many of the trends emerging as a consequence of the gig economy.

One such trend is what we are now referring to as Agile work practices. In *Forbes*, Steve Denning drew the distinction between an established company, structured to exploit as efficiently as possible the existing business model, and an Agile organisation, which he described as 'a growing, learning, adapting living organism that is in constant flux to exploit new opportunities and add new value for customers'.

The concept of Agile is to harness the energy and inspiration of employees – encouraging them to innovate and add value to customers. The process involves the formation of autonomous, self-organised teams which value, Denning says, 'transparency and continuous improvement ahead of predictability and efficiency', and recognise 'that open interactive conversations are more valuable than top-down directives'.

The idea is to stop doing any work that does not add value to the customer; as Denning concludes, 'the key to success is not to do *more work faster*. The key is to be *smarter* by generating *more value* from *less work* and delivering it *sooner*.'[20]

I must make it clear that I do not take issue with the objective of Agile as working to create innovation in a business. My concern relates to how it is implemented, and the potential for its deployment to be linked to significant changes in employment structure and conditions. Why are seemingly successful businesses not able to deliver meaningful innovation and change off the back of existing structures and without such sweeping organisational changes?

Two examples come from close to home, where Spark, the largest telco in New Zealand, recently announced it was adopting Agile as its new operating model. Denning credits the birth of Agile to a 2001 software development manifesto, and argues it has latterly become 'a huge global movement extending beyond software ... driven by the discovery that the only way for organisations to cope with today's turbulent customer-driven marketplace is to become Agile'.[21]

Spark's chief rival recognised a power move when it saw one. Not long after the leading telco signalled its Agile shift in a March 2018 media release,[22] Vodafone New Zealand announced similar plans, while neatly sidestepping any controversy by promising not to change employment contracts.[23] Subsequently Vodafone asked 2,100 of its 2,700 staff to consider voluntary redundancy.[24] Spark, on the other hand, caught heavy flak for timing its switch during a restructure and lay-offs, and for requiring 1,900 staff to either sign new, Agile contracts or leave the company.[25]

Perhaps there really is nothing new under the sun, for my observation of this debate about Agile – which is largely about employment rights and not the fundamental methodology – takes me back to Citibank and then my subsequent stint at Tower, where in both cases I was asked to take control of a turnaround situation and meld two disparate units into a new Australian wealth division. The usual difficulties were apparent, with a long-standing leadership vacuum and senior colleagues stationed in multiple cities across different countries.

The approach at Tower was made easier by my ability to bring most of my Citibank leadership with me. I was able to reinstate our daily breakfast meetings, which had some of the characteristics of yet-to-be-invented Agile work practices. We moved fast, airing issues over cups of coffee and agreeing on courses of action then and there. We implemented rapid change, separating the business from its parent and then making an initial public offering on the Australian Stock Exchange as Australian Wealth Management Limited.

Today, Agile is discussed in the context of being able to implement change quickly, often linked to technological improvements. When I look at what we achieved at Citibank and then Tower and Australian Wealth Management, it fits the definition, with new products introduced and corporate finance transactions made rapidly. The teams I led were nimble, high-functioning and wholly invested in their work. Often too invested, I admit.

What we never compromised on were the rights and autonomy of employees as defined by the law. Any concern I have about how Agile is formally deployed today overlaps with what employment law experts have expressed relative to the Spark case in particular. While Spark insists its adoption of Agile and adjustment of contracts is legally sound, commentators have raised questions about the brevity of the company's consultation period with staff and the generally untested nature of Agile in the New Zealand legal context.[26]

My experience proves rapid innovation can take place within the framework of existing employment contracts, provided there is effective leadership and communication. But does a formal shift to Agile contracts – which potentially changes the balance of power between employer and employee decisively in favour of the former – make an employee vulnerable to termination if they fail to deliver to the timetable determined by the employer, whether that deadline is reasonable or not?

Of course, all employees have performance criteria, and the four-day week is itself a productivity policy linked to output. The difference is the goals are mutually set and agreed, the contracts are exemplars of current employment legislation – and failure, if it happens, leads to loss only of the weekly day off; not the whole job.

I wonder whether, in some cases at least, Agile is not a natural evolution but a Hail Mary pass by a business in decline, or in an industry that has hit saturation point. Why did corporations that move to Agile find it such hard going before? If we look closer, we might find the real problem is inadequate leadership. Wherever Agile is adopted and a new, penalty-focused contractual model imposed, it's worth asking whether the current crop of managers and directors are all the right people for the job.

Like the four-day week, the Agile concept doesn't stop at the MD's office door. Superficially the two appear to have elements in common, if we are to trust Steve Denning's assessment that Agile 'recognizes that open interactive conversations are more valuable than top-down directives'.[27]

But Agile is too often becoming synonymous with redundancy, its drive to create business efficiency coinciding with reductions in head count, whether through voluntary redundancy or forced lay-offs. In the four-day week, the search for efficiency is designed not just to protect jobs and boost productivity and profitability but to offer workers *more* – a carrot-and-stick approach where the reward is better job security, not widespread vulnerability.

CHAPTER FOUR

The Purpose of the Four-Day Week

THE GREAT EXPERIMENT

As I have travelled the world and spoken to live audiences, media outlets and fellow leaders about my reasons for trialling a four-day week, I have reminded everyone of one thing: I am a businessman, first and foremost. My organisation is not a charity nor a social enterprise, but a typical for-profit company in which I have an ownership stake. I am responsible for the jobs and general professional welfare of 240 people, and I have to justify all big decisions to a company board. At least, that's the idea. I knew the four-day week was going to be controversial with my own board. It became slightly more controversial because I forgot to tell my fellow directors in advance, and they heard about it on national television.

In any case, the profit motive of Perpetual Guardian – a large employer by the standards of New Zealand-owned enterprises, and the country's largest statutory trust company, supervising over NZ$200 billion in assets – meant that when

I began to think about experimenting with a four-day week, I was not acting out of benevolence or a desire to be liked by my staff. I was driven by evidence-based curiosity. In that moment of enlightenment on the plane, I had been astounded and somewhat alarmed to learn that daily productivity was as low as 1.5 to 2.5 hours in some Canadian and UK workplaces. I wondered what Perpetual Guardian's average individual productivity was – we had never formally measured it.

On the back of that thought, it occurred to me that asking staff to give me a little more output in four standard days in exchange for a full day off each week might produce singularly edifying results. If everyone did 100 per cent of their work in 80 per cent of their normal hours for 100 per cent of their pay, what would happen?

The starting point for our four-day week trial was that simple. We were seeking data and we wanted to be able to compare Perpetual Guardian to companies of similar size in other markets and industries. If we were getting more – or less – done in a day than other companies, why? Initially this was merely an experiment within my own business, to establish what our approach to work was doing to my team and find out how we could work smarter.

It was only after the story broke in local, then international, media that we began to deliberately provoke a global conversation about productivity and the four-day week.

That might sound overly ambitious, but the extraordinary intensity of the interest in our trial and its aftermath told me this was a conversation whose time had come. Even before I sat down on that plane I had no doubt that the way we work today is no longer working for us.

On my return to New Zealand, I went straight to see my Head of People and Capability, Christine Brotherton, to discuss the email I had fired off to her about the *Economist* piece and my big idea. Once she understood that I was serious about experimenting with a four-day week – something I had to persuade her and the leadership team was not pie in the sky – and I was not willing to endanger the company's viability in the slightest, we talked about its purpose.

We would not pitch it to our staff as a weekly long weekend or a free day off, but as a gift in exchange for delivering productivity and meeting customer service standards, individual and team goals within the business. We explained to them we wanted to test a theory that greater efficiency would come as a result of improved staff focus and motivation, and we intended to use the business as a laboratory.

They were all in. When I explained my idea at a company-wide meeting, I was met first with stunned silence, then hesitant laughter and eventually applause. The whole team was receptive to the challenge of working differently. It was clear they understood this was not just about processes and procedures, but how they would manage their time better. It was a pact between us. If they got their work done and kept our customers happy, then I would gift them a day off each week on full pay, and they didn't have to work longer hours on the four days they were in the office. So we gave it a go.

Actions speak louder than words (or applause), and I was aware that many of my senior team leaders remained sceptical about the model. Getting their buy-in to even attempt the trial, and the need for them to keep an open mind regardless of any personal misgivings, had been an effort. Would they give it a chance and provide the leadership the trial required? Equally, would the staff respond to the challenge? Would they change work behaviours and processes to manage their time better?

There were far too many unanswered questions, yet I was optimistic that the team could deliver.

LESSONS FOR LEADERS

After a month of planning, we embarked on the trial in March 2018 with the expectation that it might not provide all the answers but could be a big step towards making our business work better for our people and for the bottom line. We knew if it worked for us – even in part – we would prove the four-day week or an alternative flexibility model could be applicable in many other companies.

In Chapter Six we will delve into how we designed and conducted the trial and later implemented the four-day week within the business, but it is important to note that a large part of the structure of the four-day week was generated by our staff, who we asked to design the trial in accordance with their individual and team workloads, performance objectives and personal schedule preferences.

We already had a modicum of data from internal staff engagement surveys conducted annually from 2015 to 2017, and this formed the basis of our pre-trial engagement scores. However, the questions were somewhat perfunctory, focusing only on how engaged an employee was with the company or how satisfied with their job, and they yielded largely super-ficial results. We quickly realised we needed expertise from outside the company. The academic researchers we invited to monitor the preparation for the trial, the trial itself and the aftermath were invaluable in securing robust data on engage-ment and a host of other metrics.

The trial was the best way to test my hunch that flexible working – in our case, the four-day week, though this book will discuss a number of alternative options – is the right thing for employers to do as the ramifications of the Fourth Industrial Revolution play out in unpredictable ways. As a businessman I want an organisation that is fiscally healthy, where there is steady growth, positive profit and loss, and channels to inno-vate and expand our platform and services into new markets. As an employer, I want the culture to be in good health, with our people being the best they can be while they're in the office and the best they can be at home. They deserve that, and so do their loved ones.

Instinctively, I felt the four-day week offered a natural solution to ills that, while they had not noticeably afflicted my company, are widespread in our culture of work. As our staff understood, productivity was the number one objective of the trial, but I also sought to find out whether we could achieve optimal work-life balance and guard against excessive stress, mental and physical health problems, presenteeism and hyperconnectedness by asking people to do more in the office in exchange for more time away from it. I was convinced the trial would help me understand whether my concerns for the well-being of my staff were justified – and whether the four-day week represented a solution.

To other employers pondering a change, I say: set your purpose first. The four-day week is only one form of flexible working, and it may not be right for every company. Be clear about what you want to achieve at every stratum, from the board to the leaders and staff. Do you want to increase engage-ment and productivity, reduce absenteeism and presenteeism, attract and keep good people, motivate your staff, achieve better overall organisational health and culture, increase rev-enue? If your objectives are explicit at the start, success and milestones can be measured accurately.

Keep asking your employees for their views. Ask them to think about, discuss and record how they will increase their own individual productivity and that of their team. This can elicit revelatory conversations about what productivity looks like – not in generic terms but *for your business*, at an individual level. This information is gold. Be prepared to invest time in this process and make decisions based on the answers you receive. For leaders and managers, this is the opportunity to take an inclusive role in committing to the initiative and guiding and coaching their teams. This engagement will build trust and have multiple benefits beyond performance. One of the most valuable outcomes is more people will find more enjoyment in their work. This enriches an enterprise far beyond what can be read on a balance sheet.

Think about how the demography of the cities and countries in which you operate is changing, and about how flexible working affects a more diverse workforce: do you have part-time employees, parents of young children, different generations of workers, people who have migrated from other countries and cultures? What do they need from the workplace structure in order to be their best at work and at home?

Most of all, be honest with yourself about what is possible in your company in its current form. Later in the book we will address the obstacles to the four-day week and flexible working, but for now, having witnessed and heard reports of failed attempts, I can say the common factors are a lack of groundwork and a top-down approach.

Unless you already have an intimate understanding of what all your staff are doing on a daily basis, what they can do better and what they want to change, you cannot unilaterally impose a four-day week and expect success. Similarly, a trial is how you find out what you don't know. Before our trial, I had spent four years painstakingly cultivating a new business and a healthy culture out of two acquired companies. This included layering digital methodologies across what was a traditional business. In some ways, we were getting sharper, but the trial exposed all kinds of old-fashioned, time-consuming duties which people had inherited from previous employees and never thought to question, so often their managers had no clear picture as to the roadblocks to productivity buried deep in the business. Once their day off was being held hostage by those unnecessarily laborious tasks, people found a way to do things better.

Remember: the four-day week is about productivity first. I cannot be more explicit than that. When people ask me about the goodwill factor of the four-day week, I remind them the feel-good part is a secondary benefit, because like it or not, our lives as we know them depend on companies turning a profit, the tax pool being topped up, and households maintaining solvency. There is an excellent case for flexible working that meets business, social and public health objectives, but it falls at the first hurdle if productivity is poor or not maintained.

The extraordinary equation of the four-day week is that by putting productivity first, and incentivising staff to do the same, the value ripples beyond the boardroom and the balance sheet to the home lives and personal well-being of workers.

IN BRIEF

- For company owners and leaders considering a four-day week, a trial is valuable. It allows you to gather data to compare your business to others of similar size in other markets and industries. And by testing the 100-80-100 model throughout the company, you can find out whether greater efficiency would come as a result of improved staff focus and motivation.

- The outcomes of the Perpetual Guardian trial proved the four-day week or an alternative flexibility model could be applicable in many other companies.

- Ideally, most of the structure of a four-day week in a given company should be generated by staff, who can design a trial in accordance with their individual and team workloads, performance objectives and personal schedule preferences. These factors will vary between organisations.

- To monitor the trial and its outcomes and generate useful data, consider engaging experts from outside the company. The academic researchers we invited to work with the Perpetual Guardian trial were able to secure robust data on engagement and a host of other metrics.

- Set your purpose first. The four-day week is only one form of flexible working, and it may not be right for every company. Be clear about what you want to achieve at every stratum, from the board to the leaders and staff. If your objectives are explicit at the start, success and milestones can be measured accurately.

- Be honest with yourself about what is possible in your company in its current form.

- Keep asking your employees for their views. Ask them to think about, discuss and record how they will increase their own individual productivity and that of their team.

CHAPTER FIVE

The Data

LET THE NUMBERS DO THE TALKING

A famous saying in business is that what's measured is managed, and as we anticipated and planned for the four-day week trial, we knew this could be the first phase of something important for our company. A key requirement was the need to prove to the board, should the trial go well, that the four-day week was a valid way of working and had long-term viability as part of the company's operations. International headlines were the last thing on my mind! Responsible and sensible boards respond to robust data (and success breeds forgiveness), so we set out to get some.

On that note, we erred in announcing the trial before amassing a comprehensive data set of pre-trial levels of engagement and work-life balance in the company. An early data set would have served as a control against the inevitable surge in engagement scores when the trial was announced and received positively by staff – so we can only make an educated guess as to the pre-announcement levels of engagement and well-being, bolstered by what staff reported to us during and immediately after the trial.

This oversight reflected the genesis of the idea – my hunch that staff members were not productive all the time, as indicated in that original *Economist* article – and my decision to test the hypothesis for myself. At first, research was an afterthought, but we quickly saw it needed to become a centrepiece of the four-day week programme.

To ensure sound methodology in the study of staff engagement levels and the impact – if any – of the trial on employee stress and well-being, we invited two academic researchers to assist with the trial: Dr Helen Delaney of the University of Auckland Business School, who conducted qualitative research into employees' experiences of the trial, and Associate Professor Jarrod Haar of Auckland University of Technology (AUT), who studied the same group of staff on a quantitative basis.

A quantitative approach is used to explain things by collecting numerical data which is then analysed using mathematical methods. This enabled us to report movements in different staff engagement variables as numbers, which could then be represented graphically for comparative purposes.

We used qualitative research to understand how and why staff members reacted the way they did – which then provided more in-depth information on behaviours. Together, the two gave a broad picture of the impact of the trial on the company.

The trial was initially set to run for six weeks, but shortly after it began we agreed with the researchers we could derive more value from the data by extending it to eight weeks. Accordingly, it ran through most of March and April 2018.

As Haar noted in his research report:

One issue with such trials is that everyone is happy and inspired [by the prospect of a four-day week] and therefore *everything* increases. Which makes determining the positive effects slightly confounded. Consequently, I included two types of constructs to test for the confidence of the data. These are variables where it is *theoretically* unlikely for them to be improved across the four-day trial.

The two he selected were 1) Proactive Personality, which reflects the personal factors which cause behaviours, rather than influences by changes in the environment; and (2) Job Complexity, which simply reflects the complexity of the tasks an employee does in their job.

A high score on the first reflects this personality trait around proactivity being more prevalent, while a high score on job complexity reflects more complexity in a person's role. These findings provide confidence and support the notion that the responses are genuine and not biased (or flawed). In essence, Haar was using these variables as control factors. Neither should move as a consequence of the trial, so if they remained stable, and other factors moved, we had evidence that the movement was a result of the trial and not, as he identified, all scores rising across the board.

Importantly, beyond detailing a set of related constructs, forming the hypotheses and finally reporting on what was found, Haar's work grounded the quantitative results of the trial in the context of other New Zealand data on the same constructs. As a leading national researcher in human resource management and organisational behaviour, he was able to reference data on 6,000+ equivalent employees from the 2017/18 period, and he told us he was confident the findings would provide useful intelligence within range of other comparison groups. In short, his analysis would tell us whether the trial made a measurable difference to the work lives and personal lives of our staff.

In Haar's data, the employee section relates to the experiences of all our staff and was collected via surveys in the week before the trial and the week following its conclusion. Supervisors were asked to provide ratings of their teams.

Though Perpetual Guardian's 240 respondents constituted a low number by quantitative research standards, the data gathering used survey techniques to determine the variation of the responses and therefore the statistical ability to detect change between pre-trial and post-trial levels, so we were able to glean a great deal from a relatively small sample size.

Haar set about selecting a series of the most appropriate variables (or types) which are used in this form of research to determine the reaction of the employees to the changes brought on by the four-day week.

FINDINGS FROM THE QUANTITATIVE RESEARCH

Section 1: Employee data

Findings: Support perceptions

Two types were selected: (1) *Perceived Organisational Support (POS)* which reflects the way employees see their organisation caring about their well-being. A high score reflects strong perceptions. There is a host of data showing this construct heavily influences employee job outcomes (satisfaction, commitment, performance, retention) and has some effect on well-being; (2) *Psychosocial Safety Climate (PSC)* which reflects worker perceptions of the way their organisation cares for their psychological health and safety, and is related to psychological well-being and engagement.

As Haar had suggested in his research report, the findings

provided support for an increase in these perceptions across the trial. While statistically significant, the increases appeared to be modest; however, this might reflect that these perceptions had already begun to be influenced (increased) around notification of the trial.

Please note that in these graphs the pre-trial average for New Zealand represents the bottom of the New Zealand data range

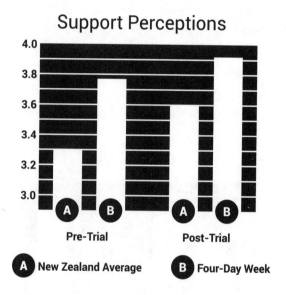

Support Perceptions

Pre-Trial   Post-Trial

A New Zealand Average   B Four-Day Week

and the post-trial average represents the top.

Haar identified that, in comparison to other New Zealand data (especially POS) the usual range would be around 3.3 to 3.6 – so we had a starting point (3.78) which was very high to begin with. The higher post-trial score of 3.91 reflects a great positive perception by employees. It was also acknowledged that the score for PSC again is quite high (by international comparison) at pre-trial and the growth post-trial is significant and high. The conclusion was that employees really thought Perpetual Guardian cared about their well-being and their psychological health and safety.

Findings: Team work

Two types were selected: (1) *Team Psychological Capital (TeamPC)* which reflects the strength of the team in regard to having hope, confidence, resilience and optimism. A high score reflects strong perceptions of these strengths within/amongst the team – not just the individual; (2) *Team Cohesion (TeamCoh)* reflects worker perceptions of the way their team operates together – how they get on and whether they are a cohesive unit. This is strongly related to performance and job outcomes (commitment, job satisfaction etc.).

Haar noted that the findings provided very strong support for an increase in these perceptions across the trial.

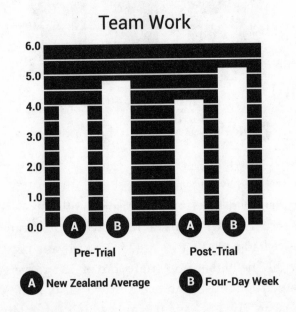

He found that in comparison to other New Zealand data the usual range would be around 4.0 to 4.1 – so the starting points (4.87 and 4.49) were high to begin with. The post-trial score of 5.19 reflected, he reported, an 'amazing' perception by employees of their psychological strength, and this was 'fairly similar' for their cohesion. In summary, employees reported their teams had grown and strengthened through the trial and exhibited greater strength because of the trial.

Findings: Readiness for change

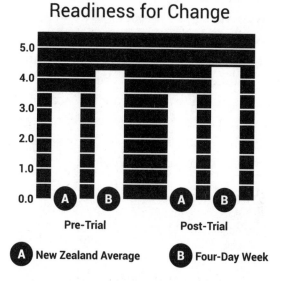

Readiness for Change

Pre-Trial — A: New Zealand Average, B: Four-Day Week
Post-Trial — A: New Zealand Average, B: Four-Day Week

Business improvement literature suggests change (like the trial) is more likely to succeed if people are positively ready (focused) on the change. This was cast at the team level for two reasons – it was felt that it was better for people to reflect upon the performance of their team rather than just themselves (more reliable), and as the trial was, in reality, mainly team-focused, this made the team approach more appropriate.

Associate Professor Haar noted that the findings provided strong support for an increase in these perceptions across the trial. Again, his comparison with other New Zealand data found the usual range would be around 3.5 (assuming a potentially positive change) – so the starting point of 4.26 reflected a high level of readiness for the trial to begin with. The post-trial score of 4.46 reflected strong growth in readiness for this change and a willingness to change to the four-day week programme. In summary, employees reported their teams were ready for the trial but afterwards were even more focused and prepared to adopt the change.

Elsewhere in this book I discuss the need for a company to be ready to embrace change as a precursor to the implementation of a four-day week. Leaders of companies that do not have a culture which is open to this should therefore consider implementing other smaller, staff-generated changes before beginning a trial. If other conditions conducive to a trial are in place, this 'pre-work' of more modest initiatives will help the culture begin to adapt to change, thereby easing the whole organisation towards a more comprehensive reordering of time and productivity in the workplace.

Findings: Work factors

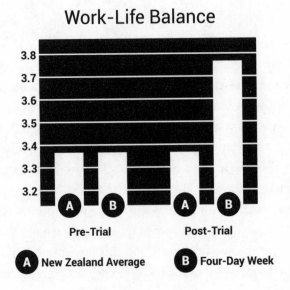

Two types were selected: (1) *Work-Life Balance (WLBal)* reflects an employee's perception of how well they balance their work and non-work roles. A high score reflects stronger balance and there is plenty of data showing this construct heavily influences employee job outcomes (job satisfaction, organisational commitment) and well-being (anxiety and depression); (2) *Work Demands (WkDemands)* reflects worker perceptions of their workload and the nature of overwork. It is linked strongly to detrimental outcomes such as lower job satisfaction and performance and lower well-being (more stress).

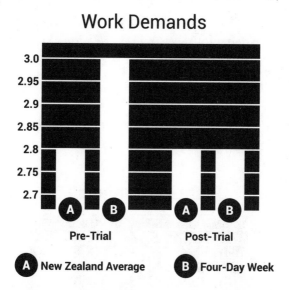

Work Demands

Pre-Trial   Post-Trial

A New Zealand Average   **B** Four-Day Week

Haar noted that the findings provided support for an increase in work-life balance perceptions across the trial. Work demands were significantly lower after the trial, which he stated reflected the encouragement to get work (37.5 hours) done in 30 hours, and psychologically this gave staff the freedom to focus on work in the four days of work time.

The trial produced a considerable amount of work-life balance data. Haar noted the starting score of 3.36 was 'quite typical' (around the usual range), although the score of 3.76 post-trial reflected a positive perception by employees, who felt a clear change in their work-life balance.

The lower post-trial score for work demands of 2.8 reflected levels more typical of other New Zealand employees. In summary, employees reported enhanced work-life balance and lower work demands, reflecting positive effects from the trial on these work factors.

Of all the outputs from the research, this was the most surprising, in that it indicated that staff were better able to handle their workloads as a consequence of the four-day week, which engendered positive behavioural changes in relation to work demands.

Findings: Team performance

Two types were selected: (1) *Team Citizenship Behaviours (TCBehav)* reflects an employee's perception of how well their

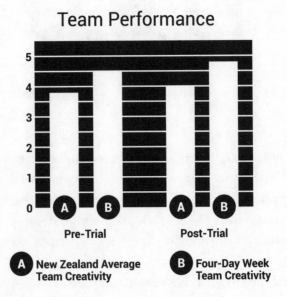

team engages in helpful work behaviours – typically things *not* in their job description and roles that are not required but help the team; (2) *Team Creativity Behaviours (TCreative)* reflects worker perceptions of how their team performs with regard to being innovative and creative.

The starting scores of 4.6 and 4.4 were quite high (typical average around 3.8 to 4.0) and might reflect the preparation done by employees and their teams in anticipation of the trial. That said, the post-trial scores reflect a positive increase in team creativity behaviours and helpful behaviours, as we would theoretically expect.

In summary, employees report enhanced team performance reflecting positive effects from the trial on work performance (at the team level).

Findings: Job attitudes

Three types were selected: (1) *Job Satisfaction (JobSat)* reflects an employee's attitude towards their satisfaction with their job; (2) *Work Engagement (Engagement)* reflects worker psychological engagement – how switched on and attuned they are to their work; (3) *Employee Retention (Retention)* reflects employee attitudes towards staying with the organisation.

The starting scores of these job attitudes were very high at 3.86 (job satisfaction), 3.97 (work engagement) and 3.94 (retention). Again, Haar speculated this might reflect that these perceptions had already begun to be influenced (increased) around the announcement of the trial to staff in January 2018. That said, they all significantly increased post-trial and these scores are very high (easily the highest Haar has seen in his New Zealand data). While coming as no surprise given the positive response to the trial announcement, employees individually reported significant positive increases in their attitude to their work.

Job Attitudes

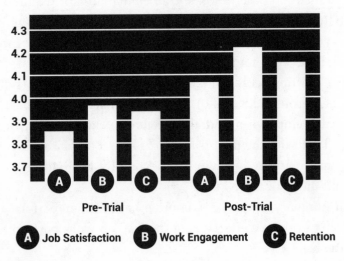

A	B	C	A	B	C

Pre-Trial   Post-Trial

A Job Satisfaction   **B** Work Engagement   **C** Retention

Findings: Well-being

Five types were selected and these all used a percentage score (0-100 per cent) – in each case, higher is better, except on job stress: (1) *Life Satisfaction (LifeSat)* reflects an employee's overall view of their life satisfaction; (2) *Health Satisfaction (HealthSat)* reflects an employee's overall view of their personal health satisfaction; (3) *Leisure Satisfaction (LeisureSat)* reflects an employee's overall satisfaction with their leisure time; (4) *Community Satisfaction (CommunitySat)* reflects an employee's overall satisfaction with their involvement with their local community; and (5) *Job Stress (Stress)* reflects on an employee's assessment of how stressed their job makes them.

The starting score of these well-being outcomes was high for life satisfaction (slightly higher than the New Zealand average of around 70 per cent). The other starting figures, at between 60 and 70 per cent, were slightly lower than we might have expected from the New Zealand data. The job stress score was similar to

Wellbeing

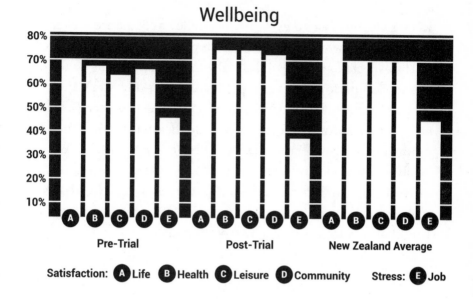

Satisfaction: **A** Life **B** Health **C** Leisure **D** Community   Stress: **E** Job

the New Zealand average (around 45 per cent). The post-trial scores reflect a solid increase in all well-being scores (and reduction in job stress). Haar commented on the strong increases in leisure satisfaction, which was interesting in the context of some of the difficulties some staff reported in coming to grips with managing and getting the most out of additional leisure time. In summary, employees reported enhanced well-being reflecting the positive effects from the trial.

Section 2: Supervisor data

Findings: Job performance

Job performance was examined using a very standard construct: *in-role performance*, which basically reflects the way the supervisor saw their employee team/s doing their job. A high score reflects strong or better performance. This type of construct is very useful when a variety of jobs are being done. It allows comparisons to be made between teams doing different types of work.

The expectation ahead of the trial was that supervisors would not see job performance go up over the four-day week trial. While this may at first glance appear perverse, it is because in effect they are working fewer days to do the same work. If they can maintain the *same* score (i.e. not drop), that would be very positive. Theoretically, there is a chance that performance could increase – as workers work harder. But given they have 20 per cent less time to do their jobs, the expectation was that there would be no increase in absolute performance.

Job Performance

Pre-Trial
Four-Day Week

Post-Trial
Four-Day Week

With a pre-test score of 4.91 and a post-test score of 4.93, Haar noted the findings provided support for no change in job performance. This would suggest that supervisors saw their team/s doing their jobs to the same standard before and after the trial, and support the notion that employees managed to do their jobs sufficiently and successfully across the four-day week trial.

Summary

In essence, the data showed that employees believed the company genuinely cared about their health and well-being, with significant improvements in teamwork, readiness for change and team performance. Work-life balance and engagement also improved significantly, but there was no discernible reduction in job performance. A majority of staff said that with the changes introduced by the trial, they were better able to do their job working four days, not five.

BETTER WORK STORIES

Dr Helen Delaney's research approach set out to provide an overview of the impacts – the benefits and challenges – of the reduced working hours arrangement on workplace behaviours, relationships and working environment, and to focus on the impacts of the trial on non-work lives. She also provided a summary of the key employee feedback regarding the possibility of implementing a reduced-hour work arrangement.

The research design involved eight focus groups with more than 40 Perpetual Guardian employees and managers, conducted between 4 and 18 May 2018. Focus groups ranged from 60 to 90 minutes in duration, and participants presented both their own experience and those of their team members. In addition, four semi-structured interviews of approximately 30 minutes each were conducted with four of the company's senior leaders.*

---

* All focus groups and interviews were conducted by Dr Delaney and undertaken following University of Auckland Human Research Ethics Committee protocols regarding anonymity and confidentiality.

Findings from the qualitative research

Impact of reduced working hours on workplace dynamics

Motivation, collaboration, productivity

In general, employees (including managers) reported the trial resulted in a number of improvements to their workplace behaviours, relationships and environment. (Table 1 in the Appendix provides a list of these improvements, with supporting quotes. See p.194.)

There were a number of persistent themes across the focus groups and interviews:

- The planning discussions before the trial commenced stimulated employees' **intellectual engagement**, because they had to think differently about their work both individually and as a team. Such discussions were new to many teams, and many employees expressed a sense of greater voice and empowerment in their work.

- The trial's planning phase resulted in many employees designing and implementing innovations and initiatives to work in a **more productive and efficient** manner. These practical micro-initiatives included automating manual processes, changes to meeting behaviour (shorter, focused, only when necessary), sharing email inboxes, phone call forwarding systems, using new smartphone applications, installing instant chat functions for team communication, and using technology to connect with clients (phone calls instead of face-to-face, to save commuting time).

- In addition to the other behavioural changes, employees combined meal breaks with work tasks, prioritised, planned and focused on work tasks, and reduced or eliminated non-work-related internet usage. An enduring theme was the increased level of focus and presence – a head-down, 'just do it' approach to one's work. The reduced hours meant that employees could sustain a more intensive work pattern, and they were more motivated upon returning to work.

- Employees reported an increase in the level of **collaboration and teamwork** directly related to the trial. They described feeling a mutual willingness to help each other out. Multiple new communication initiatives enabled a greater level of engagement between employees. Many teams (including managers) experienced greater sharing of information and/or delegation of tasks. Some managers reported feeling an increase in appreciation and trust for the ability and reliability of their team members. The trial opened managers and employees up to the idea of enabling workers to have some degree of discretion over where, how and when they work.

- Some employees described the **benefits of upskilling and cross-training**, such as feeling more challenged and stimulated by their work, together with an increased understanding of other organisational functions and a reduced risk to the organisation of losing a key person – someone who holds significant knowledge or information about the business. This notion of lower risk was raised by some employees who expressed their belief that, following the trial, the organisation as a whole was more resilient when confronted with unexpected events, such as the absence of a key person or an extreme weather event.

- A resounding theme across all focus groups was that employees had a **shared commitment to the purpose of**

the trial – and, indeed, a permanent four-day week – from a business perspective. That is, there developed a deep and broad agreement that reduced working hours can only be viable if employees meet – and, where possible, exceed – the agreed productivity measures. The trial saw an increase in motivation levels.

- Many employees viewed the reduced working hours as a gift and a privilege, not a right. Consequently they felt a deep sense of goodwill and reciprocity towards the organisation, which manifested in an openness to, they said, 'go the extra mile' and think about 'what I can do to give back'. Many employees reported a willingness to be available for work purposes on their day off.

Not all smooth sailing

While the vast majority of qualitative data details the benefits of the trial, some participants shared the challenges and frustrations that were experienced as a consequence of the four-day week trial. (Table 2 in the Appendix provides a list of these concerns, with supporting quotes. See p.200.)

Some of those shared themes included some individuals reporting an **increased feeling of stress and pressure** to complete work tasks within a shorter timeframe, especially for individuals or teams who were experiencing greater workloads (due to the time of year, a campaign, reporting requirements, reduced staff, etc.).

Certain teams/divisions were unable to fully (or partially) participate in the trial as a result. Others found themselves working compressed working hours (for example ten hours a day over four days) instead of the intended reduced working hours. Managers across all levels seemed to find it particularly difficult to reduce their working hours; as one respondent said, 'The work just doesn't stop.' Some participants questioned whether this difficulty was a result of the need to delegate more work and/or change one's habits and assumptions.

Later in this book I make the observation that one of the biggest hurdles was the attitude of management to the four-day week. Many were among the sceptics who did not believe their workload would be manageable under a reduced-hour model. I responded by mandating senior leaders to accept and use the gifted fifth day off, the same as other employees, so they would lead by example and demonstrate the value the company placed on the ultimate success of the new policy. There was, however, great variation in managers' practices despite this mandate. Some simply worked from home on the 'day off' without making this visible to their teams; others genuinely tried to take a day off but not every week; still others worked compressed weeks.

Eventually, as we worked through the four-day week trial, managers found they were consistently able to take the day away from the office, even if they used it to do a bit of homework and enjoy the benefits of some thinking time.

The next chapter's how-to guide to the four-day week explains how leaders can foster success in a productivity-focused, reduced-hour model; with most of the reported frustration stemming from perceived workload issues and increased pressure to complete work in a smaller timeframe, senior executives can step in to ensure teams are appropriately resourced such that the flexibility model is feasible for those who choose it. Likewise, the issues reported in some quarters around upskilling and innovation can be seen as opportunities for improvement by leaders who want to mitigate risk in the business and invite employees to propose solutions in areas where problem-solving and creative thinking are needed.

Impact of reduced working hours on non-work lives

Better living beyond the workplace
The data paints a clear and consistent picture of the multiple ways in which the increased non-work time improved the quality of employees' lives. The data is grouped into five main themes according to what the additional time enabled individuals to do. (Table 3 in the Appendix provides supporting evidence for each theme. See p.203.)

A consistent theme across all groups was that individuals had **more time to accomplish tasks in their personal lives** that are often, as they characterised it, 'crammed in', 'put off' or 'rushed between' in the course of a five-day work schedule.

Another dominant theme was having **more time to participate in family life**. This included working parents and grandparents being more actively involved in children's lives – sharing meals, attending day-care/school activities, talking and connecting with their children, partners, and wider family and friend networks.

Many employees (including managers) reflected on their enjoyment of having **more time to restore and reconnect**. Many reported the 'pure indulgence' of having time to themselves among the various demands of fast-paced modern life.

A smaller group of employees relayed how they had **more time to learn and contribute**. This included formal and informal study and professional development. Others dedicated the additional time to volunteer and community work.

Some employees purposefully used the **additional time to explore and imagine**. This included seeking out new travel, leisure and consumption activities they would not normally have had the time to engage in.

'What do I do with my day off?'

There were very few who reported struggles or concerns regarding the impact of the additional time on an individual's personal life. Three participants highlighted that the additional time raised existential questions about routine and security that may be initially uncomfortable. In the words of one manager, 'How do you actually spend your time when you don't have that structure around your working week?' One employee said of a co-worker that, 'She was getting a bit bored. She would have rather come to work and seen people.' Another recounted a colleague's struggle to 'figure out what to do with the day off', and said this person ultimately learned to 'spend some time with herself, which was quite an important thing to learn how to do'.

This is one of the most sobering, even depressing, outcomes of the trial – namely, the difficulty people had in adjusting to additional time off. This is discussed elsewhere in the book, but in short, it is indicative of the serious problems facing workers in the twenty-first century who have become accustomed to, and often dependent on, the stimulation of constant activity, even when that activity is unproductive or adverse to individuals' health and well-being.

In brief

- In the quantitative research the starting points of the measures of team psychological capital and cohesion rose from 4.87 and 4.49 pre-trial (already high compared with other New Zealand data) to 5.19 post-trial. Employees reported their teams had grown and strengthened through the trial and exhibited greater strength because of the trial.

- There was a high level of readiness for the trial, and the post-trial score of 4.46 (compared with 4.26 at the start) reflected strong growth in readiness for change and a willingness to change to the four-day week programme.

- The quantitative findings provided support for an increase in work-life balance perceptions across the trial. Work demands were significantly lower after the trial, and psychologically this gave staff the freedom to focus on work in the four days of work time. The starting score of 3.36 was around the usual range, although the post-trial score of 3.76 reflected a positive perception by employees, who felt a clear change in their work-life balance.

- The starting scores of 4.60 for how well teams engage in helpful work behaviours typically outside the job description, and 4.40 for innovation and creativity, increased over the trial, reflecting positive effects from the trial on work performance at the team level.

- Engagement scores rose between 30 and 40 per cent, to the highest level the researchers had ever seen in New Zealand.

- The post-trial scores reflect a solid increase in all well-being scores and reduction in job stress.

- The expectation ahead of the trial was that supervisors would not see job performance go up over the four-day week because in effect staff are working fewer days to do the same work. If they can maintain the *same* score (i.e. not drop), that would be very positive. Indeed, the findings were there was no change in job performance, supporting the notion that employees managed to do their jobs sufficiently and successfully across the four-day week trial.

- The qualitative analysis found employees were more intellectually engaged in their work, were finding ways to work more productively and efficiently, reported increased levels of collaboration and teamwork, were more challenged and stimulated by their work as they upskilled and cross-trained to cover colleagues, and were collectively committed to the purpose of the trial. Many employees felt an enhanced sense of goodwill and reciprocity towards the organisation, and reported a willingness to be available for work purposes on their day off.

- Some employees believed the trial made the organisation as a whole more resilient when confronted with unexpected events, such as the absence of a key person or an extreme weather event.

- There was an increased feeling of stress and pressure among some employees to complete work tasks within a shorter timeframe. Managers across all levels seemed to find it particularly difficult to reduce their working hours, and some participants questioned whether this difficulty was a result of the need to delegate more work and/or change one's habits and assumptions. The majority of staff said they could handle their workload better working four days, not five.

- Outside the workplace, a consistent theme was that individuals had more time to accomplish tasks in their personal lives, to participate in family life, to restore and reconnect, to learn and contribute and to explore and imagine.

THE PROFIT MOTIVE

Every competent board member knows the most crucial measures of their performance, at least in ordinary economic times, are the productivity and profitability of the company they govern. For my part, I am certain that the promise of the four-day week must go beyond the metric of employee engagement, job satisfaction and well-being to be recognised as the defining model of the future of work; we have to prove that companies' bottom lines will be enhanced by a productivity-focused, reduced-hour model.

It was the case with Perpetual Guardian. I was the sole shareholder when the company was founded and for several years afterwards, but by 2018, when we trialled and implemented a four-day week, another shareholder was in the mix. Had we not been able to prove the four-day week made the business more efficient *and* more profitable, it would not have been a viable proposition. What we discovered was that a relatively modest amount of requisite additional expenditure to meet the customer service needs of our smaller-staffed branch offices was offset by the many collective savings made by almost all staff, who identified the time-wasting habits that could be eliminated.

The truism that time is money is truer than ever for a services-based business like ours, and a pure focus on productivity, supported by a clear-eyed dismissal of virtually every business practice that undermined individual output – such as overlong meetings, workplace interruptions and unnecessary processes – led directly to an upswing in profitability.

Our overall profitability rose during the trial period, and we have since seen company revenue and profitability increase by 6 per cent and 12.5 per cent respectively. These improvements demonstrate that the implementation of the four-day productivity week policy has had no adverse impact on the performance of the business, and they prove that productivity increased. And although the increase in revenue (which in our business is largely linked to external factors such as markets and demographics) was relatively modest, profitability per employee – a base measure of overall productivity – increased by 14.5 per cent.

A further benefit for the business has been the material improvement in brand recognition. Our research has indicated that our brand awareness increased by more than 30 per cent, with our profile as a leading and trusted brand increasing by 48 per cent and 37 per cent respectively. Our share of voice in media has averaged over 80 per cent against our competitors in our domestic market.

But don't take my word for it. A 2019 study of 250 UK businesses operating with a four-day week calculated that the participating companies had together already made an estimated annual saving of £92 billion.[1] The white paper by Henley Business School at the University of Reading found 'a shorter working week (on full pay) could add to businesses' bottom lines through increased staff productivity and an uplift in staff physical and mental health', along with other benefits.

We do not have to pore over these companies' profit and loss reports to see where the profitability boosts are coming from. If staff are more productive, as two-thirds of the businesses confirm, and generally healthier (62 per cent of firms reported fewer sick days), then profitability would be expected to rise. Quite simply, those working in the businesses are getting more useful work done and costing the firms less in wasted hours at work and absenteeism. The companies are also in a position to invest in the necessary assets for future profit-making, with 63 per cent of employers reporting the four-day week had helped them attract and retain talent.

The Henley report authors were unequivocal as to the bright

prospects for the model as a causative factor in business success: '[T]he four-day week trend shows no sign of slowing down. Over a third of business leaders surveyed (34 per cent), and nearly half (46 per cent) of those in larger businesses, say making the switch to a four-day working week will be important for future business success, so we're likely to see more trials and implementations in the coming years.'[2]

One such trial was the grist for a research report led by London market research agency The Mix. The report, authored by Strategy of Mind, recounted The Mix's own experience with a four-day week. From October 2017 to October 2018, the company remodelled its working week and asked staff to work standard hours from Monday to Thursday and take Fridays off – at full pay. (The difference between this model and that of Perpetual Guardian is that The Mix did not intend to maintain a typical five-day week schedule in terms of availability to clients, as is generally expected of professional services firms.)

After one year of a four-day week, revenue at The Mix was up 57 per cent, client numbers doubled and new client referrals were up 50 per cent, and though there was no increase in productivity (which the agency measured by overall profitability), there was also no decline, despite the hard reduction in work hours of a full day each week. Staff absenteeism and sick days were down 75 per cent.

All things being equal, I would expect revenue, client business and staff attendance levels of this magnitude to ultimately translate to increased profitability, especially if the company can keep finding ways to enhance the focus on productive and billable activity. As the report authors said, 'There is a strong case for reducing paid working time for all workers so that four days becomes the new "normal".'[3]

FAILURE *IS* AN OPTION (AND EVEN A NECESSITY)

The outcomes of the trial exceeded our expectations, and indeed any predictions, by a considerable margin. The trial was valuable in that it empowered our staff and gave us a metric for gauging the output of every role and team, and because it provided a useful pool of quantitative evidence, along with the candid feedback of scores of staff, to present to the board as part of the case for a productivity-focused, reduced-hour work week on a long-term basis.

By all reasonable measures, our trial worked beautifully, but it was not an unqualified success. The trial taught us that we cannot talk about a four-day week as a new work construct unless we can admit the possibility of failure – and if there is one thing most company founders and bosses have in common, it is a horror at failure of any kind. Generally speaking, what most CEOs do on a daily basis is less paradigm-shifting and more prosaic, and much of the motivation, especially if your job could be on the line, is around trying not to stuff things up.

That fear – 'What will this cost us if it goes wrong?' – is probably the four-day week's biggest obstacle. It is also an asset. Any business leader with a serious intention to reinvent how work is done in their sphere by introducing a flexibility policy must first accept that failure is an option, and even a tool of progress.

I'll give you an example from our trial. After we made the company-wide announcement, our teams had about a month to strategise how they could meet their usual outputs while giving each member a weekly day off. The glitches that could impede success were addressed before and during the trial, mostly within teams and occasionally at a higher management level.

I describe the trial as a 'qualified' success because it included a notable failure, which proved highly instructive. It was in a part of the business staffed by about twelve people who had joined the Perpetual Guardian group of companies through acquisition, but had never become entirely integrated with the company. This team was based in a separate site, and was led by a founder who maintained a prominent leadership role in the business. A general manager had been appointed to take over from the founder and bring the company fully into the group, but it was early days and doubts were already mounting about this manager's performance.

Why did the four-day week fail in this team? The team members found they were unable to meet the service standards expected by their customers, and with half the team away on Friday and the other half on Monday, productivity was not maintained. There were no apparent changes in work behaviour on the other four days to make up for the day off taken by each member. In short, it was the opposite of the result I intended for the four-day week.

Conversely, the rest of our staff, embedded as they were in our culture and ethos since Perpetual Guardian's founding four years earlier, understood immediately this was not about everyone taking a three-day weekend. They knew they would need to be creative and find ways to compromise. Their managers were ensuring everyone knew it wasn't a case of 'You take Friday off – I'll take Monday!', and maintaining customer service levels was paramount. If a team's plan would risk any customer having a less-than-stellar experience as a result of the four-day week, they would have to change the plan.

The team that failed had not yet embraced this ethos, and lacked a manager who could direct the members away from the appealing and expedient route of three-day weekends for everyone. Based on our analysis, there was simply a lack of forethought and planning, and a failure to collaborate as a team to see how they could focus the eight-week trial on the dual goals of productivity and customer satisfaction. Other employees knew that cutting corners was never going to be appropriate. It was a standout failure, and one I attribute to culture and leadership.

This is proof the onus rests evenly upon managers and workers. Both groups are responsible for honouring the obligations of the four-day week. If the team is underperforming, and the employer/manager tolerates repeated productivity shortages without revoking the four-day week privilege from a team which has not delivered on its promises, other teams will – in light of the lack of sanction – likewise renege on their agreed terms of performance, and the benefits of the four-day week policy will be lost.

It is not uncommon for promising workplace initiatives to flounder due to a lack of consistent leadership. Sometimes, the top brass aren't sufficiently committed, or they're easily distracted, and they change tack or get cold feet. On other occasions, the costs and benefits of the initiative are not fully understood by middle and senior managers who lack a clear incentive to invest in the policy and sell it to their teams. Any flexibility policy can only be effective with continuous work and attention to areas of vulnerability, and, as with so much in life, it is easier to lapse back into old, conventional habits than persist in challenging the status quo.

Once management is invested, workers need to do their part by recognising the 'gift' of the policy and adhering to its conditions and principles. The culture that forms around the flexibility policy must include a shared understanding that it is incumbent upon team members to call out colleagues who are abusing the process, and a mutual dedication to constant review of work practices to forestall regression to previous bad, unproductive habits.

Any flexibility policy or trial should be entered into with a company-wide understanding that failure to deliver on productivity goals, and subsequent failure to remedy this, will result in a removal of the four-day week and a reversion to five days. At that point, regardless of the reasons for failure, the venture again becomes a shared challenge and an opportunity for management and employees to clear a path to reinstitute the four-day week as expeditiously as possible. Protracted failure might be a sign of either unrealistic goal-setting or management backsliding on its commitment.

With the lessons of failure and a redoubling of efforts, there is a realistic promise of success – and importantly, the failure of a flexibility policy doesn't mean the policy is moribund. In fact, it is proof of life, a positive sign the policy is viable and is being taken seriously by all parties. Failure, followed by reinstitution, represents a reaffirmation of the policy and maintains its health and relevance.

CHAPTER SIX

How It Is Done

PREPARE THE GROUND

In business as in life, sometimes you have to take a leap. At its heart, the four-day week is a compact between the owners, leaders and employees of a business. Preparing properly for a four-day week in your organisation will help every party honour the compact, get the best out of the new way of working, and make it a viable long-term programme for the company.

First, build trust

The four-day week is an employee-led process where the magic bullet is trust. Years ago, in a difficult leadership role at Citibank in Australia, I found a good way to get the best from other people is to treat them as peers. This is important because no person has a monopoly on good ideas, and a team often knows the intricacies of the business – and certainly its processes – better than the leader does. Even before that, in my

Royal Navy days, I learned another valuable rule: never ask someone to do something you wouldn't do yourself. All of this came into play during the trial.

The conditions which made the trial possible weren't formed overnight. Before my ownership of the two companies which became Perpetual Guardian, the people in those enterprises had endured prolonged and tumultuous change, and there was a degree of insecurity. Over the four years preceding the trial we turned the culture around gradually, through activities such as a branch renewal programme, which, while it meant some HR changes, was a tangible sign we were investing in the business and not just indulging in a restructure. People saw any temporary instability was in service of something much better.

By the time we announced the trial, I had proved to our staff time and again they could trust me and believe what I told them. They knew I did not have an authoritarian style, and when I said I wanted them to lead the programme and tell their managers anything pertinent, I meant it, and they were safe to speak freely.

Staff were also assured there were no secret deniers or ostriches (more on these later) among the leadership team. Everyone made a commitment based on my insistence that our strategy would work as long as we all gave it everything we had.

Trust is the essence of good culture, and any leader considering the four-day week has to be honest about whether the culture is ready. Do staff trust their higher-ups to back them when they make suggestions about how the business can work better? Do the senior managers and CEO have a reputation for standing by their word and cultivating a supportive environment? Without trust, the balance among the staff between supporters/adopters and cynics/detractors will tip towards the latter, probably with disastrous consequences for the policy.

No business is perfect, but a four-day week will not work as a palliative for serious ills in the culture or operations of a company, and a failed attempt will likely make morale worse. In a culture without open communication and trust, even a leader with the best intentions is likely to find those are misinterpreted, with staff suspecting a ruse to tweak work conditions for the worse. Likewise, if staff do not enter a trial in good faith, having each made a personal commitment to change their work behaviour, there will be no improvement in productivity and the four-day week will fail.

Don't overthink it

Start with the core principles of the four-day week, crystallised by the 100-80-100 rule (100 per cent of the pay, 80 per cent of the time but delivering 100 per cent of agreed productivity). People are only required to work for four days provided that they meet productivity targets agreed with their managers. They work the usual length of day and they are paid their usual salary. The value to employers is that they are paying for a certain level of productivity – so, in theory, if a given employee delivers that while taking one day off a week, both they and their boss should be happy with the arrangement.

It is a carrot-and-stick approach. Staff remain contractually obligated to work five days, at least until employment legislation catches up to flexible working, a sticking point we will discuss later in this book. In that context, the day off is a gift. There is no backsliding. If productivity drops from the agreed level for no acceptable reason, the gift is withdrawn and the five-day model is reinstated.

Every employee at every level is eligible for the productivity (or flexibility) policy, the most senior managers included. This sends an important signal to the whole organisation: there are no hidden costs or negative outcomes – such as loss of career advancement, compensation or responsibilities – from using the policy.

Equally, in environments where the four-day week is on offer, anyone has the right to decline that construct and propose a personal flexibility policy to suit their circumstances better, such as a five-day week with truncated hours. Remember: the point is productivity, and within that framework, many things are possible. There is no one perfect destination or one right way to get there.

As we have identified, it is all too easy, when considering a change in company policy which has the potential to remake many aspects of your culture and operations, to overthink it – to mentally play every angle in a bid to identify wrinkles in the plan and forestall errors. I can put you at ease right now: you will make mistakes. Whether you start with a trial or dive right into a productivity policy, you will discover aspects of your operations – individuals and perhaps entire teams – that aren't functioning nearly as well as you thought. You will probably find fallow patches of time wastage and unproductivity in some areas. None of those are reasons not to proceed – in fact, quite the opposite.

Two companies I met with as they were planning the four-day week are instructive. To my horror, the first company, after analysing every possible variable and trying to conceive of every possible pitfall and corresponding solution, had deemed Friday was the least productive day. Accordingly, it was proposing a policy with a predetermined structure of three-day weekends every week, to be trialled over a six-month period.

I was alarmed by this approach because it wholly contravened our philosophy and advice, which was to ask the staff how they would structure the policy and the trial. Additionally, our experience suggested that a fixed day off every week just didn't work in terms of meeting and maintaining customer service standards. The four-day week is explicitly not designed to give every staff member a three-day weekend, unless this can be achieved without compromising productivity, profitability or the needs of customers. My gut feeling as I left the meeting was that they wouldn't proceed with the policy.

A few weeks later we heard that as they were so unconfident about their ability to persuade the management and board to implement the policy, it was abandoned. In effect, they had thought themselves right out of the four-day week.

On the same day, I met with another company. On receiving my advice to hand the challenge over to the staff and just try it, they brought forward the date of the trial. They understood that, at least initially, the bulk of the productivity benefits in the trial phase would come from behavioural changes rather than differences in policy or process. They also got the point that the four-day week is a process driven by workers, not managers – bottom up, not top down. The ability to not over-think it was a relief to the managers charged with designing and implementing the trial.

Most CEOs consider themselves good problem solvers, and many would attribute their career ascension to their skill at putting out metaphorical corporate fires, at least in part. Facing the prospect of introducing a four-day week, they have a strong tendency to evaluate risk, identify problems and design solutions. Their approach is usually evidence-based, so – in theory – the management team is buttressed by a comprehensive plan for success.

What could possibly go wrong? With this approach – almost everything.

In all the planning, all the environmental scanning and

poring over research, CEOs forget to ask their employees how the policy might work. After all, why should they? They're great problem solvers! However, for the 100-80-100 model to roll out effectively, the employees have to own the policy. The employees themselves have to name the barriers to success and find the ways to break them down. They must not be out-thought or outplayed by senior managers who think they know better.

Run a trial. Or don't

Refer to the previous section. At some point you have to stop ruminating and take a leap. If you are reading this as a corporate leader, you should already have a sound grasp of your company's culture and its strengths and shortcomings. What you might not know so well is what all your staff consider to be the possibilities within the company.

If you haven't previously or recently invited your employees to present their ideas about how the enterprise can evolve or improve, asked them how they can find more efficiencies in their work days, or consulted them as to whether they feel their responsibilities are balanced fairly against those of their colleagues or team members, a trial is a great way to tease out this information. It is a safe space for everyone to put forward the good, the bad and the ugly about how the company works and what can be better in the company and its people. You are guaranteed to lift the lid on practices and problems which, if handled well, can be beneficial to the organisation, without your staff worrying about making themselves redundant.

At Perpetual Guardian, we conceived the idea of a trial and promptly made the announcement to staff, accompanied by a memo in which we set out the objectives:

To undertake a company-wide trial of working a four-day week (as opposed to a five-day week) with all staff receiving the 'fifth day' of each week as a paid day off in order to:

- Generate an empowered, engaged and staff-led discussion and focus on respective team and individual productivity; and
- Understand if increased working flexibility and the opportunity to spend more quality time with family and pursuing personal interests is valued such that it not only increases overall staff engagement, but specifically also results in increased productivity.

You can see what we did there: as soon as we announced the trial, staff understood their role in it. They were expected to contribute both ideas and effort, and to approach it as a test of productivity. It was closely associated with work flexibility and the opportunity to take more personal time, but without the productivity factor, the benefits would be lost.

None of this is to say a trial is a mandatory part of introducing a four-day week or any other flexibility policy in a given company. The particular set of conditions our company faced at the time of the trial in early 2018 were commonplace but not ubiquitous. There will be company leaders who have a better grasp of individual and team productivity than we did at the time. There will be companies with lower head count and a single location (we have more than a dozen branches) which may find it easier to consult internally, design and implement a flexibility policy than to go through a trial – but care must be taken. As we have identified, the trial represents a safe space for innovative ideas. Too much prior planning can kill the initiative.

Embrace time as the scarce resource

With few exceptions, at the top of the business tree the plaudits and the biggest bucks are reserved for leaders who focus, often at the expense of all else, on improving the profitability and productivity of their companies.

Mostly, expert consultants are hired to engineer these improvements, and cutting costs and staff is a common tactic. The business leader who takes the advice to reduce headcount is treating money as the scarce resource – and to protect it, expenditure must be reduced. This has the advantage that the path to improved profitability is well trodden and recognised, and represents a low-risk strategy for management.

This approach is not necessarily designed to raise the overall productivity levels of the business, and the remaining workforce is likely more constrained by the recent reduction in numbers of staff. This may not be immediately damaging to output on a per-person basis, because which company is truly 100 per cent productive at all times, with workers delivering maximum productivity every hour they are in the workplace? While these traditional cost-cutting or process improvement methodologies can and do raise profitability and productivity, the boosts often come at the cost of the morale of the workforce, and do not on a long-term basis address the underlying barriers to productivity within the workforce itself.

Allowing for the additional costs of retaining the consultants and doing the restructure, the effect on the company is a bit like a double-shot espresso or a chocolate bar on a weary person – a surge of energy followed by a reversion to the previous state.

The CEOs and boards who are still using this approach are stuck in the last century, along with the five-day week. They are devoted to a top-down style of business improvement, and any consultation with staff – such as when redundancies are in the offing – is prompted by a mix of lip service and legal obligation.

The absolute opposite approach is the four-day week productivity policy, which makes *time* the scarce resource by posing the challenge to the existing workforce to deliver their current productivity in four days rather than five. Staff are not threatened with lay-offs but presented with the opportunity to raise productivity and reduce operating costs by finding and addressing any barriers to productivity in their own behaviour. They are encouraged to point out anything that might unduly soak up their precious time and prevent them from achieving their productivity targets and enjoying the four-day week.

Taken one by one, these little hindrances would be unlikely to attract the attention of a management consultant, but when identified and fixed, they have a significant and cumulative effect.

The time-centric model also recognises even the most productive person is not always working at 100 per cent capacity. The first objective of the policy is to raise the productive percentage of the work day by incentivising the employee to change their own behaviours by reducing the time they devote to unproductive or work-avoidant activities, from social media use to overlong meetings. As I discuss below, there is evidence that an ideal productivity-to-break ratio for the human brain is 52 minutes to 17, leaving plenty of time in the work day for personal business which does not threaten productivity goals.

Crucially, by making time the scarce resource, the

employees also identify process barriers to productivity – things that could make it difficult to hit productivity targets and negatively impact their experience of the four-day week.

In a given company, this collective exercise in self-reflection can deliver the bulk, if not all, of the productivity improvements necessary to make the four-day week a success. At the same time, it ensures productivity measures are established for all roles, which delivers a considerable benefit for future operations.

Trust is a factor here. In receiving liberty from management to find solutions to roadblocks in any aspect of how the company runs, employees must feel safe to disclose ways of doing business activities more efficiently. The four-day week means they do not have to fear making fixes will render any jobs redundant; instead, they are helping to ensure the promised reward of 80 per cent time in the office is claimed.

Do your homework

Before we began our four-day week trial, we made one good decision: we initiated independent research to demonstrate the validity of the exercise. This meant even if everything turned to custard, we would emerge with a better understanding of our company, its culture and productivity. As much as anything, we needed to generate data from the trial which would satisfy our independent directors and the representatives of our private capital partners that the policy had quantifiable benefits.

If we made an error in the process, it was starting with only a limited programme of staff surveys in the year before the trial was announced, so the canvassing of workplace mood, job satisfaction and other metrics was not as comprehensive as I would have liked. This restricted the before-and-after view of the company to a fairly narrow set of data linked to staff engagement. Of course, at the time this data was being gathered, the four-day week had yet to be conceived.

In hindsight, we compounded the misdemeanour by finalising the scope of the research only after we had announced the trial, and our base scores were consequently skewed somewhat by the positive mood that arose in the company with the announcement. We would have amassed more accurate historical data had we started the thorough surveying earlier, and established the base point before beginning to discuss the trial. The outcome isn't disastrous – the lack of previous scope merely means our results probably underestimate the positive impact of the trial on company morale and staff engagement.

The key lesson here is to make sure you have done comprehensive staff surveys *before* announcing the trial, and that you are clear as to the key variables you will need to use to convince management, directors and other stakeholders of the trial's success. These can then be evaluated during and after the trial – and accurate improvements can be recorded and reported.

As was canvassed in the previous chapter, an early decision was made to run two forms of research alongside the trial. Once it became apparent there was considerable external interest in the trial, we committed to making the research available to third parties to inform other workplace decision-making and encourage debate about the merits of the four-day week for the modern global workforce.

Even if you opt not to run a trial, for a four-day week or other flexibility policy to be introduced successfully, independent research has to be an integral part of the programme in my view. You can expect to find, as we did, that academics working in the fields of sociology, business and management will be eager to assess in real time the effects of a large-scale productivity and engagement experiment on an everyday workforce.

Count on the concept being hotly debated, probably controversial, and in all likelihood strongly resisted by some directors and members of the management team. But facts win cases, and it was difficult for the sceptics among our leaders to dismiss or refute the overwhelmingly positive findings of the research – especially when combined with a productivity rate consistent with pre-trial outputs.

Consult your lawyers

We sought legal advice before the trial and again before we implemented the four-day week on an opt-in basis. In our pre-trial memo to staff, we explained:

> We have sought advice from our employment lawyers. In summary, by conducting the four-day week trial, we are not changing terms and conditions of employment under the Employment Relations Act (2000) or the Holidays Act 2003. It's important to note the four-day week trial is exactly that: a trial. We will revert to our normal working weeks (as per we are contracted) after the trial ends.

Because what we were proposing had never been done inside the New Zealand legislative framework, we had to be sure we could offer a four-day week, even temporarily, and stay within the law. Quite understandably, our staff wanted to know they weren't unwittingly forgoing leave entitlements or other benefits by participating in the trial.

We were able to offer the four-day week by treating the day off as a 'gift' in exchange for the agreed output from the employee, who would accrue annual leave and other entitlements as normal, because apart from the reduction from 40 to 32 hours, there were no changes in their terms of work. It was a work around which allowed us to proceed but is unsatisfactory on a long-term basis, especially as other enterprises follow suit. We will explore this as one of the obstacles to the four-day week in Chapter Nine.

Though momentum is building behind the four-day week, the model as we conceived it is still rare in practice, and with employment law being hugely variable between jurisdictions, I strongly encourage every company leader considering a flexibility policy to seek a legal opinion on their proposed solution so as to avoid any unexpected consequences.

GO TIME

The rules for running an effective trial and productivity policy are surprisingly simple. Create the conditions for your people to do their best – but understand not everyone will respond to those conditions in a similar fashion.

Do not disturb

For productivity to go up, disruption must come down. I'm corrupting the old saying, but it gets to the heart of the problem in many busy, noisy, connected workplaces. In Chapter Ten we will discuss the problem of the open-plan office.

To understand how environment affects output, think of

productivity as if it were a bank account: a good night's sleep is a deposit; so is a brisk walk in the sun, a cup of coffee from an expert barista, and an airy, comfortable office with plenty of natural light. What drains the account and chips away at the productivity of workers? Anything that constitutes an interruption, from phone calls and text messages to email alerts and unscheduled face-to-face conversations with colleagues.

On that basis, it might be a minor miracle to achieve high productivity in a regular work day. A 2018 online survey of hundreds of users of RescueTime, a time management software company, found that nearly 52 per cent of respondents were interrupted frequently while working, and 64 per cent said their most common – and most distracting – interruption was of the face-to-face kind, for example, a co-worker stopping at their desk.[1]

As the survey also identified, those direct interruptions are the hardest to ignore. When a colleague is standing in front of you asking a question, refusing to respond is an act of hostility and would likely lead to bigger difficulties in the workplace. Email likewise plays an unhelpful role in relation to productivity, but is a less overt distraction, with most respondents agreeing inbox messages are the easiest form of interruption to ignore.

Author and leadership expert Mark Murphy analysed the results of a quiz by his company LeadershipIQ about time management. Based on more than 6,000 responses, Murphy discovered 71 per cent of people report frequent interruptions while at work[2] – significantly higher than the figure determined by RescueTime, which canvassed a smaller group of people.

Regular interruptions have ramifications for more than productivity, and can reach into the psychological realm. As Murphy writes: '[w]hen people get interrupted frequently, there's only a 44 per cent chance that they'll leave feeling like "today was a really successful day". By contrast, when people can block out interruptions at work, there's a 67 per cent chance' they will feel the day was a success.[3] It stands to reason if more than half of people who endure frequent workplace interruptions leave work feeling negative or frustrated about their day, it could engender a sense of job dissatisfaction – 'Why can't I be allowed to do what I was hired to do?' – and even spill over into other aspects of their lives.

Conversely, a day-to-day feeling of accomplishment, fed by the freedom to get work done with little to no unscheduled interruption, is likely to give rise to an overarching feeling of job satisfaction, goodwill towards colleagues and clients, and a belief the workplace is structured and managed in a way which elicits people's best efforts and productive energy.

It is easy to impose some practical rules for creating an office environment conducive to output and which discourages repeated distractions. There was one, stunningly simple, anti-interruption device that proved highly effective in allowing people to make the most of their four days a week in the office and meet their productivity targets during the Perpetual Guardian trial: a miniature flag. When this little object was placed upright in the pencil pot on a worker's desk, it signalled that the person was concentrating on a task and was not to be disturbed.

Other workplaces use a kind of traffic-light system, where everyone has a little light on their desk. When the light is on, no interruptions are allowed. In some environments, workers will don headphones to signal 'do not disturb', and a good noise-cancelling device will not only eliminate the distracting hum of the office but let the worker listen to creativity-stoking background music, or do work-related viewing or listening, without disturbing others.

Other ideas for discouraging interruptions, submitted by RescueTime users, include:

- Changing the notification settings on smartphones.

- Using the Do Not Disturb mode in apps.

- Physically separating from co-workers (using a closed-off office or meeting room, or working from a remote space such as a coffee shop or home office).

- Scheduling 'heads down' time.

- Telling co-workers who approach that you are busy and will talk later.[4]

Murphy calculates it takes ten minutes to clear the mind and get engaged in a big task such as writing a report – so every interruption potentially costs ten minutes of productive time while the worker gets reoriented to the task and regathers their train of thought. His simple fix involves blocking out times during the work day by turning off email for a set period; putting the phone somewhere out of reach; and using a physical barrier such as an office door, or working away from your usual space, so others can't easily interrupt.[5]

In almost every workplace, solving the productivity puzzle means first winning the war on technology by inverting its use to enable output, not disrupt it. Don the headphones or place a flag in the pencil pot, disconnect the email and switch on Do Not Disturb on the phone, set a break reminder, and let the work flow.

Harness the power of concentration to put productivity first

If workers are having trouble concentrating on the job, it is likewise all too easy for employers to misunderstand how work flexibility can be a solution to poor productivity. Most of the conversation about flexibility focuses on the work-life balance benefits, and treats the improvement of productivity as a by-product of the policy. That is, a reduction in working hours generates higher productivity as a consequence of a better work-life balance.

There is conclusive evidence to support this assumption, including a 2009 analysis by the National Bureau of Economic Research in the United States which suggested an interactive symbiosis between productivity and work-life balance (WLB): '[W]ell managed firms tend to be more productive and more energy efficient . . . better managed firms also have better WLB practices.'[6]

Despite the data, boards and senior managers are inclined to encounter the four-day week as if it were a risky proposition. They fear either the anticipated benefits to productivity will not accrue, or the workforce will – sooner or later – give up its initial enthusiasm for the project, and productivity will revert to the norm. Workers, for their part, tend to worry that the flexible working arrangement is merely a ruse to reduce pay and benefits.

The Perpetual Guardian four-day week offsets these risks by making productivity, not work-life balance, the point of concentration. This is what differentiated our policy from many that had been attempted previously, and it was the driver of success in every metric, from employee satisfaction to company revenue. Indeed, the four-day week policy was referred to internally as the 'productivity week policy'.

Based on this core agreement between management and staff to deliver mutually agreed levels of productivity in four days rather than five, everyone understood their role and responsibility within the trial, and everyone stood to benefit in tangible ways.

The purpose of our pre-trial planning period was to determine the measures of productivity to be applied to individual teams. I have to admit, before the trial we lacked adequate productivity measures across some of our business units. Ironically, even if the trial had failed spectacularly, we would have emerged with a greatly enhanced understanding of the dynamics and appropriate performance benchmarks necessary for the efficient running of the company.

I would venture the same is true for many companies. If so, a trial will at least produce a comprehensive picture of appropriate output for each team or worker, which can only be to the advantage of boards and shareholders who are constantly seeking valuable insights about their business or investment. If all parties enter a trial knowing the mandatory outcome is the maintenance of standard company productivity, the exercise is much easier for the CEO to defend and for boards to justify to shareholders. When the concentration is on output, and output does not change, there is no adverse impact on the economics of the organisation from implementing the policy.

Experiment with the 52/17 ratio

For company leaders, communicating these boundaries to staff should be straightforward. Employees will need to get the appropriate permission to change their workspace or make themselves unavailable during normal work hours – but there is plenty of data a worker can use to make their case, such as research by the social networking company the Draugiem Group, which used the time-tracking productivity app DeskTime to examine the habits of the most productive users.

'What they found,' reports Lisa Evans in *Fast Company*, 'was that the 10 per cent of employees with the highest productivity surprisingly didn't put in longer hours than anyone else. In fact, they didn't even work full eight-hour days. What they did do was take regular breaks. Specifically, they took 17-minute breaks for every 52 minutes of work.' Importantly, those breaks were often spent away from the computer, whether in work-related conversation or taking a walk.[7]

Is the 52/17 rule the ideal work structure? Evidence that structured short breaks correlate with higher productivity also comes from a 1999 Cornell University project which used a computer programme to remind workers to stop for a break. According to *The Atlantic*, researchers concluded 'workers receiving the alert [reminding them to stop working] were 13 per cent more accurate on average in their work than co-workers who were not reminded'.[8]

The key point here is an emphasis on productivity doesn't mean no social interaction in a normal eight-hour day, including lunch. The 52-17 model of a work day still represents 102 minutes of downtime plus a lunch break.

Let the people lead . . .

The good news? The most important ingredient contributing to the success of a four-day week or other flexibility policy is already present in your workplace: your people.

On a Friday in early February 2018, I announced the four-day week trial in an all-hands meeting with a video link to our national branches, and told staff the trial would be collaborative, not prescriptive. No one was going to tell them what to do, and we would need to figure out the answers together, in their teams and with their managers. Success would depend on how well we shared ideas, troubleshot problems and asked for help.

I opened numerous channels for communication, from our internal website to informal gatherings such as staff drinks, so staff could make suggestions in whichever forum felt most comfortable. Staff understood they were being brought into the process early, that I had a hunch but didn't know how to make it work, and I needed their ideas and advice. Of course, this all goes back to trust; they knew they would be listened to and respected.

Based on my experience, I advise other leaders to give employees a reasonable amount of time to think about how they can work differently, and encourage them to come up with their own measure of productivity. Ask them to decide how they can organise time off within teams while still meeting customer and business imperatives. If the trial is to work, it must start with every employee having clear individual and team goals.

The engagement of staff in this way is not only crucial but scrupulously fair, because only those responsible for output can determine how they will deliver on the agreed productivity measures. A prescriptive approach which does not invite the employee to redesign their own work structure would be mistaken; it stifles engagement and ownership of the whole process.

By challenging the employee to conceive ideas for improvements to maintain and even raise productivity, the company circumvents obvious issues with systems and processes which would prevent or hinder productivity improvement.

In a top-down process, leaders run the risk of the whole

policy being viewed as the Homeric 'Greeks bearing gifts' – that is, the staff perceive the project as unachievable, disingenuous in intent and destined to fail, and the company is likely to be perceived as having attempted a flexibility policy to score a cheap public relations win.

... but make sure you know your people

To say workers will respond to news of a four-day week policy in one of a few predictable ways is not a generalisation but an evidence-based assessment of human psychology and how we respond to unexpected change.

The internal announcement of a four-day week trial or policy will shake leaders and workers up, challenge their assumptions and work habits and probably make them think about their work in ways they never have before.

For the purposes of this discussion, I am referring to employees with a standard full-time contract, with standard benefits and entitlements, in companies in established industries – as opposed to start-up operations in newer sectors which may have attracted talent with flexi-enticements such as unlimited annual leave.

When we talk about a company culture that will either permit or forbid a four-day week, we are talking about four kinds of workers. You have worked with all of them, and you are one of them. Some companies have many of one and only a handful of another – but in preparing to implement a new, flexible structure, each of these types must be understood, with appropriate strategies adopted to accommodate their needs and preconceptions.

1. **THE ADAPTIVE ENTHUSIAST**

In any company, some staff will receive the announcement of a four-day week policy as though all their
Christmases have come at once. They will understand and
embrace what is being offered, and adapt seamlessly to
the new model of work. In most workplaces, these individuals are likely to comprise the minority. This is also
likely to include parents returning to the workforce who
know, and have already demonstrated, that they can do a
full week's work in four days. They will probably be the
policy's biggest advocates.

2. **THE DOUBTER**

Typically, the most resounding response will be from
those who comprehend the structure and the benefits
but are convinced there is a catch. Why, they will ask,
would any boss choose to cut the working week by a full
day unless they have an ulterior motive? Is this a ploy to
reduce staff numbers? Will productivity targets be raised
once we have proved we can work more efficiently over
four days?

These are legitimate questions for which leaders need
to be prepared – and the doubt will be greater and more
urgent in companies which have recently (in the previous
two years or so) been subject to merger or acquisition.
Few experienced workers in established industries have
not endured one, or indeed several, restructures, and the
doubter will be looking for reassurance that the four-day
week is not code for downsizing. I previously discussed
the job losses which followed the introduction of Agile
working at two large New Zealand companies – this is a
real issue which must be acknowledged and addressed
upfront and with honesty and integrity.

3. **THE REFUSENIK**

A third group of workers will be wholly opposed to a four-day week. For some people, the collegial interaction they get each work day is central to their social pattern, and they are loath to lose any part of it. Others will be flummoxed by the suggestion that they can or should complete their week's work in four days, not five. Some of the people in each of these subgroups may come around if presented with other flexibility options, such as working five shorter days instead of four eight-hour days – but those who prefer the status quo, and perform well within it, should be respected and accommodated.

4. **THE NON-COMPROMISER**

Finally, there are the people who will welcome the four-day week while failing to recognise its benefits are attached to responsibilities. These workers focus solely on the upside for them, but are unable or unwilling to contemplate changing how they work in order to deliver the productivity increase that is a prerequisite for the policy's adoption. In such cases, the skills of senior leaders and team managers must be brought to bear so the non-compromiser does not disrupt the opportunity for colleagues who are more open-minded and collaborative.

Now let's move up the ladder to the C-suite. The attitude from this domain sets the tone for the company conversation and provides direction for the rest of the leadership team. Like employees, managers can also be categorised into broad groupings. Though the CEO is the central figure, with unparalleled influence over the entire enterprise, these 'types' can of course be found at all levels of management as well as on the board. Failure to recognise and address the issues they raise will lead to failure of the initiative.

1. **THE DENIER**

Whenever I talk about the merits of the four-day week anywhere in the world, a member of the audience will rise to their feet and utter a variation of, 'That's all well and good, but it wouldn't work in my business.' The denier has decided that the policy *cannot* work, and is overlooking the golden rule of the four-day week: ask the staff.

During my announcement of the four-day week initiative, I freely admitted I had no idea how to effect the policy I had in mind, but it was aspirational and I wanted the staff to tell me what had to change to make it happen. Before the trial, I am sure everyone in the company would have said success wasn't possible.

Of course, the denier may be right. The form of the four-day week we have adopted at Perpetual Guardian is not the only solution, and companies will identify the form of flexible working that works for them. But a refusal to countenance an open and honest trial of alternatives suggests a mind closed not only to a four-day week but also to any new ways of working and doing business.

This is a problem because the work revolution is coming, ready or not. Refusal to explore the possibilities will deprive a company of talent. Hanging on to the old ways of doing things will probably be the harbinger of failure.

There is, sadly, no way to circumvent a denier. In the absence of strong leadership and advocacy the four-day week policy is destined to fail. The denier can then neatly close the loop with, 'I told you so.'

Deniers below CEO level can be managed, not least

because they can be benchmarked against other leaders who embrace the policy. Although there may be exceptions, a failure to successfully implement the policy will usually identify a failure of leadership. Such individuals can be performance-managed towards the desired results.

Boards faced with CEO deniers should consider whether this is a symptom of more comprehensive limitations, such as a refusal to experiment, to communicate openly and honestly with staff, and to keep an open mind. There is only one solution: get another CEO.

2. THE OSTRICH

Ostrich leaders are everywhere. These are the managers who don't believe the conversation is necessary, because everything is just fine as it is. It is pure complacency.

Boards and CEOs confronting an ostrich should be armed with the reams of data showing the beneficial impact of flexible working policies on productivity and engagement, staff retention and sick days.

Our own experience identified significant opportunities for process improvement and not inconsiderable shifts in time management for better productivity. At the least, this can be an inexpensive process improvement whose benefits are clear even to an ostrich.

3. THE BAD SALESMAN

This is the leader who embraces the concept of the four-day week but is uncertain about the reaction they will receive from senior managers, their board of directors, and their shareholders. Their visible doubt means the pitch, if it happens at all, is less than convincing.

When we designed our trial, we had to convince ourselves first. Yes, the four-day week was a hunch and my entrepreneurial streak means I have some of a gambler's instincts, but I owned a significant proportion of the business and I wasn't going to put my company, and my wallet, on a roulette wheel. We convinced ourselves of the viability of a trial by running it on the basis of productivity, and we backed this up with independent research and agreed productivity objectives.

These metrics, along with the explicit promise to withdraw the gift of the four-day week in the event of poor productivity, should placate the most recalcitrant of boards, and give confidence to the poorest of salesmen.

Watch out for the habits of 'highly productive' people

Within most medium-to-large businesses is a cadre of employees who are certain that they are already highly productive and working to capacity. These folks will view the implementation of a four-day week more as an imposition than a gift, because the suggestion a four-day week can improve productivity will be seen as preposterous. For these employees, a reduction in hours will mean work is just not done; their days are already full.

The data, not to mention general workplace observation, tells us some employees are more productive and some less. Nevertheless, it is highly unlikely any individual is working at maximum efficiency and to full capacity, on genuinely productive tasks, at all times.

Managers of the 'highly productive' worker who is resistant to a review of actual productivity will have to lead the worker along a different path, starting with questioning whether every process or task undertaken by the employee is a) productive,

b) necessary and/or c) could not be achieved faster with an improvement to the process.

I would wager even the most efficient employee can find ways to streamline processes and curtail the ostensibly productive yet practically unproductive activities which plague many workplaces, from overlong and overstaffed meetings to unnecessary email chains. These give the illusion of productivity but add little or nothing to company output and profit.

Be willing to withdraw

The commitment to a four-day week has to be more than skin-deep. The leader who introduces a flexibility policy from a popularity motive will not achieve the necessary outcomes. At the heart of the introduction must lie a serious discussion about productivity improvements. The leader must be willing to make the possibly unpopular point to their people that productivity is not a by-product but the main event, and everything else, including work-life balance, is secondary – but if it's done right, the balance will come.

The harsh truth, and this must be explained to employees upfront, is failure to maintain productivity at the mutually agreed levels will result in the loss of the four-day week. This will not win any popularity contests, but leaders must be willing to use the sanction of withdrawal.

The four-day week is yet to be trialled widely across industries and different markets, but I expect those leaders who prepare the ground properly, begin the exercise with open and honest conversations, run a staff-led process, and are not motivated by a need for popularity will rarely have to exercise the sanction.

Allow people to opt in

To be consistent with the four-day week's design as a staff-led initiative, any decision by management and the board to introduce it on a long-term basis cannot be imposed unilaterally across the business. Staff must be consulted and allowed to opt in or out of the putative new work structure.

In the case of Perpetual Guardian, we were legally permitted to gift a weekly day off on a long-term basis only if we allowed staff to opt in. But it is also the logical decision, because as any trial is likely to prove, the four-day week is not the optimal work structure for every person. When I say 'opt in', I mean a literal and simple process where staff fill out a form, approved by lawyers, which commits them to a four-day week. Terms are clearly stated, including the fact that all their usual employment conditions, responsibilities and benefits apply. Their employment contracts, signed when they first joined the company, remain unchanged.

The productivity measures agreed for those opting in must be set in advance and approved by their manager, and the opt-in policy itself is not open-ended, but renewable after twelve months, pending a comprehensive review of those measures led by the employee and completed before the year is up.

Some workers will prefer to work a five-day week and negotiate reduced daily hours to free them up to do school drop-off or pick-up. For others, work is an important part of their social life and they prefer a five-day schedule, again possibly with reduced hours. There is another, probably quite small, cohort which needs a full 40-hour week to achieve their productivity objectives.

Importantly, the opt-in model lets companies accommodate the seasonal fluctuations which affect most businesses. For example, in our company there are peak periods when our accounting team is working long hours and a four-day week is not practical – indeed, it would cause more stress. For those whose work pattern isn't consistent, consider the times of year when more flexibility can be offered, and how this can balance the ledger against the periods when everyone is going full-tilt.

OUT OF OFFICE

One of the most common questions directed at me in the global four-day week conversation is, How does it work for non-office-based businesses? Those who run or work in roster-based, rush-hour industries such as retail and hospitality often do not see how a four-day week model can apply to them.

Take a retail store. How many times have you gone into a shop and been studiously ignored, or were served by someone who was clearly unhappy in their work? Are those people productive? No.

Now, there is already shift work (an established form of flexible working arrangement) at play in retail, because many shops are open seven days but most workers have weekly days off. If you are a retail owner, can you calculate whether a fresher workforce might have better sales performance? If you gave people more choice as to when they worked, might you find you have some workers who are keen on, say, a Friday or Saturday shift, which may be a period of time when one of their colleagues doesn't want to work? The example mentioned in Chapter Three, showing how giving staff some shift flexibility improved sales at a Gap store, is instructive.

If all staff were consulted as to how they wanted to structure their work week – what works best for their lifestyle, study schedule, childcare responsibilities and so on – might you get a better performer than the exhausted, over-it worker who cannot summon the energy to cheerfully serve a customer? It is likely that staff retention would also improve.

Hospitality is not dissimilar. How many of us have had bad service in a restaurant? If a chef is working every hour God sends, can we expect the rate of food production, or the quality, to be consistently good? What I tell other leaders and business owners is to play the long game. In roster-based businesses or those when business traffic is highest on evenings and weekends, the four-day week is entirely possible, but there is likely to be a cost increase in the short term because more employees will be needed.

But remember: the four-day model is about output, and if people are fresher and more enthused, might they upsell on a bottle of wine? Might they suggest the perfect belt to go with that new dress?

In any industry, a jaded worker is not a good thing. Someone who is better rested, doesn't take sick days, has good mental health and the time to balance home and work is, I believe, going to be more productive. To focus purely on cost – or input – is to miscalculate, and miss the point.

IN BRIEF

- To prepare the ground for the four-day week, build trust, don't overthink it, consider running a short trial, embrace time as the scarce resource, do your homework, and ensure you obtain appropriate legal advice.

- Once a trial or productivity policy is established, find ways to reduce disruption and distractions in the work environment, such as objects workers can display to signal that they would prefer not to be interrupted.

- Concentrate on the value of output to ensure the business objectives are widely understood from employee to board level, and experiment with models of working which incorporate regular breaks.

- Let the trial and policy be led by those who will implement them – the workers – and understand that not all managers or employees will embrace or find it easy to adapt to a productivity policy. It may not suit all staff, making an opt-in model necessary.

- Workers must understand from the outset that failure to maintain productivity at the mutually agreed levels will result in the loss of the four-day week.

- The four-day week is just as viable in non-office-based businesses; it is simply a matter of starting by consulting staff as to the work week structure which works best for their life outside work.

CHAPTER SEVEN

The Broader Benefits

PORTRAIT OF A SUSTAINABLE PLANET

Though for the purposes of this book I am focusing on productivity at a workplace level, even modest improvements to national productivity have the potential to generate vast macroeconomic benefits. According to the UK-based New Economics Foundation, a work week of 21 hours could help address a 'range of urgent, interlinked problems', including 'overwork, unemployment, over-consumption, high carbon emissions, low well-being, entrenched inequalities, and the lack of time to live sustainably, to care for each other, and simply to enjoy life'.[1]

This assumes, of course, a shorter but more productive work week is capable of supporting an individual's income needs. The Perpetual Guardian case proves it can be done.

Let's zoom in to my adopted home city of Auckland, New Zealand, and float a theory. Say the four-day week catches on, and organisations across the city cut down on their daily in-office head count by 20 per cent. The number of cars on the road each day drops by at least a fifth, and by up to 40 per cent if parents are routinely permitted to work five shorter days and do school drop-off and pick-up.

A 2017 report by the New Zealand Institute for Economic Research on the benefits from Auckland road decongestion means we know exactly what this decrease in traffic volume would mean for the city's economy.

The report found that productivity could be boosted by at least NZ$1.3 billion per annum (1.4 per cent of Auckland's GDP) if use of the road network could be optimised. Additionally, if the average speed across the Auckland network was close to or equal to the speed limit (known as free-flow), the benefits of decongestion during week-days were estimated at around NZ$3.5 million per day, or between NZ$1.4 and $1.9 billion (between 1.5 and 2 per cent of Auckland's GDP).[2] Imagine these results extrapolated for New York City or London or Buenos Aires.

In Chapter One I discussed the intensity of congestion and the lengthening of commutes as a by-product of the way we work today, with billions of hours, dollars, fuel gallons and pounds of carbon dioxide expended each year in developed countries, where the term 'rush hour' has been part of the lexicon for as long as anyone can remember. Even if we leave aside the climate change question and apply a pure economic lens, a widespread model of working which prioritises product-ivity and efficiency over a robotic adherence to working hours (which were once dictated by the sun and are now mostly arbitrary) is a no-brainer.

When we do turn our minds to the welfare of the planet, the answer is just as obvious. A 2018 article out of the HR department of UC Davis bluntly makes the environmental case against work inflexibility: 'Not going into work could be one of the most environmentally sustainable things you can do as an individual employee.'[3]

Examining the putative benefits of flexible working arrangements, or FWAs, from an American standpoint, the author notes the two main contributors to US greenhouse gas emissions are transportation (29 per cent) and electricity production (28 per cent), with about 135 million Americans commuting to work. Fifty per cent of those workers have jobs they could do remotely some of the time, and the emissions-reduction value of those workers avoiding their normal commute on half of their usual work days is equivalent to removing 10 million cars from the road.[4]

The FWA programme at UC Davis has helped 'increase worker productivity and retention and enhance work-life balance', with the primary options specified as flexitime (altering the start or end times of the work day); a compressed week of fewer, longer days at work; and remote working for part of the week. Every option means skipping the commute and/or evading rush hour at least some of the time.

Bolstering the UC Davis case is the study by Henley Business School at the University of Reading which found that, in addition to the positive effects on productivity and the physical and mental health of staff, a reduced-hour work week promotes environmental sustainability. The report's authors said, 'The four-day week also demonstrates a positive impact on the environment, as employees estimate they would drive 557.8 million fewer miles per week on average, leading to fewer transport emissions.'[5]

Remember, the Henley research, while significant in the existing literature, incorporated data from only around 250 businesses which reported doing a reduced-hour four-day week. If we extrapolate the reported employee commuting behaviour across the UK and even the whole developed world, there is indubitably a strong case for the modification of worker transportation via a four-day week as a tool to protect the climate and forestall catastrophic change.

This case is bolstered by a study published in the *Review of Political Economy* in 2018. Researchers from Colorado State University, New College of Florida and Dickinson College in Pennsylvania analysed data from the US Bureau of Economic Analysis and Bureau of Labour Statistics and found households with longer work hours have significantly larger carbon footprints.[6]

As I write this, Extinction Rebellion is blocking key roads around the world to argue the case for governments to take immediate steps to become carbon neutral. This has drawn comment on the significant negative effect a carbon-neutral stance could have on a country's productivity and global competitiveness. Yet a widespread four-day week could immediately achieve a substantial reduction in pollution levels without any adverse impact on business performance.

The four-day week can be an answer to crises big and small – from climatic instability to work-related stress – if we are prepared to let the data lead us into action as a global collective. A productivity-focused, reduced-hour model of work is far from the only measure needed to achieve and preserve planetary sustainability, but the evidence shows us the intensification of work in the digital age has had either a neutral or a deleterious effect on every metric save the creation of wealth. Even then it is only a minority of individuals and corporations that are getting vastly richer – and they live under the same volatile sun as the rest of us.

I am not selling a fairy tale in saying it is possible to create a virtuous circle, one in which people, economies and the planet are healthy, by modifying the standard work week to focus on productivity and well-being. Just as every employee has a responsibility to make the four-day week work within their company, we have come to understand only lately that the climate crisis is not someone else's to fix – we are all in this

together. What if we start by making relatively minor individual changes to work patterns and schedules but on a large
scale, just as we did with recycling our household waste? That
part of the solution is so simple has to come as a relief.

WORKING FOR GOOD

The value of the four-day week is not only in its potential to
de-stress people and the planet, but also in a condition we
attached to the Perpetual Guardian productivity policy. Those
who opt in are required to give one of their gifted days off to
charity every quarter. They can choose what they would like
to support, and we specify only that they volunteer in some
way. Each employee in our company donating their time four
days a year adds up to about 1,000 days of socially good activity annually.

To my mind, this obligation to donate a day each quarter
reinforces the idea the four-day week itself is a gift, and serves
as a reminder of the policy's objective to enable people to be
the best they can be at work and at home. Contributing to the
community is part of this.

Volunteering New Zealand, for instance, advocates for flexible paid work as a way into volunteering. The organisation
posits there is measurable value to the worker, their employer
and the community in having the support of paid work to
undertake unfunded activities that range from the urgent,
such as volunteer firefighting, to the prosaic, like caring for
an elderly relative.[7] In all cases, the value adds up, with flexible working arrangements creating time savings that can be
redirected to non-profit organisations and worthy causes.

Policy conditions aside, the genuine enthusiasm of Perpetual
Guardian's staff to do volunteer work validates social exchange

theory, which suggests, according to the School of Social Work at Tulane University, that 'a relationship between two people is created through a process of cost-benefit analysis. In other words, it's a metric designed to determine the effort poured in by an individual in a person-to-person relationship.'[8] The theory can be applied to friendships and romantic relationships, and to workplace exchanges too – chiefly between employer and worker, with each party calculating the give and take, and whether continuing the professional relationship is worth it to them.[9]

A worker in a toxic environment who is being underpaid or not recognised for their efforts is likely to throw in the towel. Conversely, someone who is being given the 100-80-100 option of working is not only likely to hold up their end of the bargain but is likely to want to give extra in exchange for the perceived value of work flexibility. Volunteer work becomes part of the exchange.

For the business, the rewards come in different forms, including a competitive advantage. Though we did not plan it, the announcement of the four-day week eventually was integrated into our marketing strategy, and the independent charitable work done by staff dovetails with our company's large-scale philanthropy services. During the trial, our market share grew and we won more contracts, and the positive notoriety has increased alongside the global four-day week conversation.

Back to that virtuous circle: let's predict a world in which governments begin to legislate for a four-day week, or at least incentivise businesses to offer a flexible work model while protecting the established rights of workers. A common condition of that legislation or reward system might be something resembling Perpetual Guardian's policy – each worker is required to spend one day each quarter contributing to the greater good.

What if companies were rewarded for steering their workers towards causes that advanced sustainability? Can we envision a situation in which companies band together across whole cities to have thousands of workers volunteering in environmental clean-ups, planting trees, working in animal shelters and rescue facilities, and even undertaking further education in sustainability issues?

Part of the future of work must involve leveraging corporate and worker power in the service of climate stability. This can only happen through some form of accord between government and business.

In France, Emmanuel Macron's commitment to the reintroduction of a form of national service provides a glimpse as to how this might manifest. He is proposing a two-phase national service covering all 16-year-olds. The first would be a one-month placement with a focus on civic culture, possibly through voluntary teaching and charity work, and the second a placement of between three months and a year in which young people could opt for volunteer work in heritage, environment or social care. (Both placements were intended by Macron to have a military component, but the BBC reports this has been watered down following pushback by youth organisations.)[10]

The benefits of a four-day week are myriad, and their effects can be intensified and accelerated through standard legislative means. This is where the pool of data emerging from businesses in multiple industries, cities and countries is increasingly valuable. Governments can use the evidence base to support a new model of work which does not involve a compromise on the accepted economic benefits of industry but can deliver huge returns in the form of individual well-being and a broader contribution to the collective good.

TWO WOMEN

The gender pay gap, discrimination and a lack of diversity remain entrenched problems in the twenty-first-century workforce, with some of the worst examples being found in the biggest American tech and gig companies, as commentators such as Susan Fowler and Dan Lyons have highlighted.

A lack of flexibility in work is usually perceived to be more harmful to women, who are more likely than men to put their careers on hold to care for children. Yet the opposite has also been proved to be true, with some analyses finding flexible working arrangements are more advantageous, and accessible, to men.

A 2014 Furman University study of flexible working from a gender perspective found that men who asked for a flexible schedule were more likely to be granted their request than women. A 2016 study by German researchers, again comparing male and female employees, identified that though workers with schedule autonomy earned more than those working standard hours, '[m]en with schedule autonomy earned 6,700 more euros per year than men with fixed schedules, while women with the same autonomy earned just 2,000 euros more per year than women with traditional schedules.'[11]

Plus ça change. David Burkus, an associate professor of management who analysed the findings, theorised that men desire flexibility because it helps them be more productive, whereas flexibility helps women manage childcare responsibilities. Looked at from another equally plausible angle, Burkus said women may be subject to the biased view among their peers that they can *only* want flexible schedules to meet family demands, and not to be more productive.[12]

Regretfully, sexist discrimination persists in spite of the millions of women who are every bit as, or more, committed to their work as their male colleagues. Two anecdotes about Perpetual Guardian illustrate the potential for the four-day week to narrow the gender pay gap and rebalance the scales of work and family, for women and for men.

The family-friendly merits of the four-day week are evident in stories like that of Greta Lambert (whose name has been changed to protect her privacy). Greta is a Perpetual Guardian staff member who worked on the design and implementation of the four-day week policy. She is married to a chef who usually works the second half of the week and on weekends. After the trial and the analysis, when it became apparent the four-day week was likely to become a fixture in our business, Greta and her husband decided to start a family.

The difference the four-day week made in the structure of their lives, permitting them to have a day off together each week, meant having a child was viable. In a country with – like every other developed nation – a declining birth rate, a young couple made a monumental life decision as a consequence of a flexibility policy that is agnostic as to the gender, parental status or future family plans of workers.

Greta's parental leave entitlements are contractually protected apart from the flexibility policy, and if she resumes her current role after having a child and chooses to negotiate a new working arrangement, she will do so based on output, not hours in the office.

Remember Christine Brotherton, our HR director who was instrumental in designing and refining the four-day week policy? In some respects, she was the unwitting guinea pig for it. When Christine joined the company at the beginning of 2016 she came into a role that had been advertised as full-time, but for a variety of reasons she negotiated to work a four-day week. This meant she took a lower salary and lesser benefits than an equivalent full-time worker. To Christine's thinking, this was standard, and as a senior HR leader she knew the industry norms as well as anyone.

When I looked at Christine's output, though, I saw that what we agreed might have been standard, but it certainly wasn't fair. In four days a week, she was just as productive as a full-time employee. I told Christine I was increasing her salary and benefits, and she continued to do 100 per cent of the work in 80 per cent of the time.

The initial agreement Christine made about her employment package is exactly what women (and their employers) should avoid. Women who become mothers typically leave the workforce for a time, and when they come back, they may negotiate a shorter week, but they usually still deliver the same output as a full-time employee. Instead of negotiating on time, workers of any gender and parental status should negotiate on output, which is the first measure of value for an employer who is focusing on the right things.

If the employer's top priority is hours, the highly productive woman who has to leave mid-afternoon to collect her child from nursery is going to be devalued against the worker who routinely shows up for a nine to five but does two hours of useful work in an average day.

If every worker was able to negotiate on productivity, not time, the gender pay gap would diminish rapidly. You have to wonder why any company owner or leader would be opposed to this equation, because it guarantees they get exactly what they pay for. Christine's story is the four-day week policy in microcosm for working mothers; in treating them as full-time employees by recognising their productivity, it signals that they can work four days a week and still advance their careers. Thus the gap shrinks – not just in compensation but also in disparity of representation of men and women at the highest levels of business and governance.

There are dozens of stories like Christine's and Greta's in our company. Some of the best testaments came from fathers who wanted to be more involved with their children's lives, and the four-day week made that possible. This is not an incidental matter; gender stereotypes will persist if men continue to work full-time and women do not. The mere fact of fathers spending more time at home, without compromising on income or career prospects, changes expectations about the division of domestic labour and the role of women in the paid workforce.

Christine Brotherton's take on the four-day week

The aim of the four-day week trial was to determine whether the 'carrot' of having one day off per week at full pay was sufficient to encourage our staff to think quite differently about how they were working.

Based on our experience, the biggest piece of advice we have for anyone considering introducing a similar policy is to be clear about your objectives and what you are trying to achieve. It's also important to be bold, and to have an idea and see it through. Often companies can get stuck in the technical aspects of how to implement a new policy.

Be collaborative in designing a flexibility trial or policy. Leadership is crucial to success, but a flexibility policy is unlikely to work as a top-down or authoritarian construct. The success of our trial came from empowering staff to come to their own decisions and to trust them to make the right call with regards to their customers and team members.

We created a policy that could flex depending on workloads, projects or customer requirements, and there were times when staff didn't take the 'rest' day. But we empowered staff to make that decision themselves as to whether it was the right thing to do. It's important for leaders and managers to take a coaching and supporting role as opposed to being directive.

Another critical aspect of the policy is coming up with productivity measures individualised for different people and parts of the business. The trial enabled us to have a deep conversation with each staff member so they could understand what their value was in terms of output. It helped everyone to become conscious and deliberate about what they were doing and why they were doing it.

One of the many initiatives that came from staff was to cut meeting times from 60 to 30 minutes. At the end of the trial we measured whether there had been any loss in output or value from the shortened meetings. There was not. Staff became more deliberate about their behaviour and started ensuring they had an agenda for meetings and were thinking about how they were going to work together and respect each other's time.

From the beginning of the trial, we ensured staff didn't extend the hours of their four work days, but stuck to their normal contracted hours. The policy was about focusing on work efficiencies in order to get an extra day off.

The trial showed us traditional ways of working and regulated hours of work are becoming less relevant in today's society. The four-day week gives workers the gift of time to look after themselves and reconnect with their families, and we know well-designed flexibility and productivity policies like this are starting to make a difference in people's lives.

We encourage other businesses around the world to adopt this innovative thinking and look at new ways of working that focus on output, not time, to move away from the traditional nine-to-five (or longer) way of working. After all, if we continue to do what we've always done, how are we going to remain relevant and do things better in the future?

MINDING THE GAP

Families make many decisions based on economic outcomes. When two people earning roughly the same incomes have a baby, the mother is more likely to take time off, which means the father needs to work harder so they can make ends meet. Perhaps he seeks a promotion to bump up his pay. If he's successful, they no longer earn the same, and it is rational for them to prioritise his career. In perpetuating the nineteenth-century construct of the five-day week, we have created a world of work which reinforces the gender pay gap and the gendered division of labour at home.

Indeed, the way we got to the five-day week in the first place was on the basis of a division of labour in heteronormative relationships. With few exceptions, as the middle class swelled in the post-war years of the twentieth century, women looked after the home and men went to work, with families comfortably supported by a single income. The public and private spheres were separate and their management strictly delineated. In the modern world, they are no longer separate.

The gender pay gap

What remain divided, often without justification, are the compensation levels of men and women in the workforce. The average gender pay gap across OECD countries was 13.8 per

Gender pay gap by country

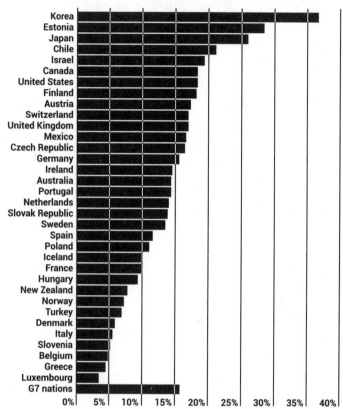

cent, with the US and Canada both sitting above average, at 18.2 per cent, and other developed and developing nations skewing from as low as 1.5 per cent (Romania) to the peak of 34.6 per cent (Korea). When self-employed people are measured, the US tops the list with a gender pay gap of 56 per cent, and New Zealand and Canada rise to 33.9 and 34.9 per cent respectively.[13]

As the second decade of the twenty-first century draws to a close, we are working from the advantageous position of having identified the existence of a gap in how men and women are compensated. We have tracked the parameters of that gap across industries and markets, and forced an acknowledgement from governments, corporations and employers that this form of economic discrimination is materially destructive to a diverse workforce and to the interests of women and families.

Current UK statistics indicate there is no material pay gap between men and women up until around the age of 40 (prime time for women to become the predominant carers of young children and elderly parents). In midlife it starts to jump, rising to 12.8 per cent in the 40 to 49 age bracket and 15.5 per cent among 50- to 59-year-olds.[14] This indicates that a compensation methodology linked to time in the office rather than output will inevitably lead to pay disparity, even in cases where women are as productive as their male counterparts.

Finding balance through productivity

Its focus on output makes the four-day week part of the solution. The typical work patterns and performance rewards of corporations prevent men from being the best dads they can be and hinder the career progression of women who are primary caregivers. As long as the time-based approach to work remains the standard, this cannot improve much.

Recognising this, many firms – while stopping short of trialling or adopting a four-day week outright – are now focusing on improving the gender balance, closing the pay gap and offering more flexibility to allow for family and childcare obligations. Flexible working arrangements are allowing more people to become employable, and employers to draw from a deeper pool of talent, with work-from-home arrangements offering paid work to skilled women and men who are caring for young children. Technology facilitates remote conference calls and webinars, and organisational cohesion is maintained by periodic face-to-face meetings with the team.

I fear there is an inherently ad-hoc bent to these arrangements, which in many cases are based on the argument of the individual worker that flexibility in *their* case will benefit the company. Better for workers and companies is a truly comprehensive approach, one which frees up some of the time of all of the people by setting a base productivity level. This can directly reduce gender inequality in personal labour and professional compensation. It can help couples find balance in their personal responsibilities and save some money on childcare.

In particular, productivity-based flexibility removes many of the obstacles that have historically prevented women from ascending to senior levels of business and governance in the same numbers as men.

In our experience at Perpetual Guardian, the four-day week empowered staff to make decisions and also gave them a collective ownership of the future of work. It is evidence of how this work model levels the playing field for all workers, because compensation is negotiated on productivity. Differences in gender, ethnicity, age and even work history are irrelevant, as long as the worker is qualified for, and capable in, their assigned role.

We have created a world of work which reinforces the gender pay gap and the gendered division of labour at home.

The four-day week proves definitively there is no need to resort to gigs and zero-hour contracts, and risk losing hard-fought-for protections for workers. The companies which persist in this behaviour are intent on milking every last drop of human capital.

Less stress, more output

Earlier in this book I discussed rising rates of work-related illness, including depression and anxiety. The so-called hustle culture and hyperconnectedness that are products of the digital age are intensifying as the gig economy grows. Workers fear their job or industry will become obsolete, and workplaces are overtaken by a collective nervous energy that drives people ever harder. We have more than enough evidence showing this approach to work causes burnout, demoralises culture and erodes productivity.

In the UK in 2017/2018, 595,000 workers suffered from work-related stress, depression or anxiety, and 15.4 million working days were lost.[15] The human cost of mental illness that can be traced directly to workplace conditions is horrific. It is unconscionable. If you removed empathy from the equation and considered the data only from an economic perspective, to leave these conditions unchanged would be idiocy.

The Perpetual Guardian trial amassed data which proves workers can be as productive in 32 hours as 40, but less prone to stress-related illness or mental illness stemming from work. Other companies experimenting with the work week schedule are finding comparable proof. Though the productivity programme by Melbourne digital agency Versa is not exactly like our own, in that their hours are slightly longer, the company has found by closing its doors on Wednesdays and asking staff to work 37.5 hours over the other four days, its people are happier, less stressed and more productive. The business is three times more profitable than it was in early 2018, when the work week changed, and revenue has grown by 30 to 40 per cent.

Chief executive Kathryn Blackman told ABC that she understood why other firms would be resistant to a 'radical' idea like a four-day week. 'It comes down to one word, and that's fear. And I think that's fear of having to trust your own staff – that they're going to do the right thing.'[16]

Can you trust your staff to work a four-day week? There is only one way to find out. As with the environmental argument, the logic is so obvious it hardly warrants debate: enable people to, within reason, set their own hours on a productivity basis and they have more time available for self-care. Functioning at a higher level, they can give more to their work.

I know the four-day week represents a big call for CEOs who have to rationalise the policy to directors and shareholders. Effectively, employees are given a 20 per cent pay rise. The first Fortune 500 leader who pulls it off will make corporate history. But the incontrovertible truth is it makes massive business sense. Do a trial and you will find sick days drop, output and profitability will rise, job applications will increase and resignations will go down, if they don't cease altogether. People will be noticeably less stressed, and the calibre of work will improve across the business.

IN BRIEF

- Decreasing overall traffic volumes as a result of the four-day week may contribute to a significant reduction in carbon emissions and in lost productivity as a consequence of commuting. Most flexible working arrangements mean skipping the commute and/or evading rush hour at least some of the time.

- The Perpetual Guardian productivity policy specifies that each employee who opts in donates one of their gifted days each quarter to an activity for social good. Flexible working arrangements extend social and economic value by creating time savings that can be redirected to non-profit organisations and worthy causes.

- Social exchange theory supports the idea that a worker being given the four-day week is likely to want to give extra effort in exchange for the perceived value of work flexibility. Volunteer work becomes part of the exchange.

- The four-day week has the potential to narrow the gender pay gap and create a more equal division of labour between women and men at work and at home.

- The story of Christine Brotherton, the HR director who helped develop the four-day week policy, proves its benefits for working mothers; in treating them as full-time employees by recognising their productivity, it signals that they can work four days a week and still advance their careers. Likewise, it helps male workers be the best dads they can be without making career sacrifices.

- There is mounting evidence to show that workers can be as productive in 32 hours as 40, but are less prone to stress-related illness or mental illness stemming from work.

CHAPTER EIGHT

The Importance of Being Flexible

BASECAMP: A DIFFERENT KIND OF UNICORN

Opponents of the four-day week – the refuseniks and deniers who say it cannot work across industries, or that it leads to a short-term boost followed by a backslide – might be sceptical about the real effects of a productivity-based work schedule on health and well-being. They need not worry. As Chapter Five demonstrates, the positive effect of the four-day week on the lives, bodies and minds of our 240 staff is both anecdotal and evidence-based, and we continue to track these metrics as the programme rolls into its second year.

The whole experiment started with a hunch we would get better outputs as a consequence of having a more engaged, less stressed, loyal workforce which was working four standard days instead of five. I already knew, from my decades at the top of the cut-throat corporate tree, people work better when they are empowered, engaged, stimulated, acknowledged for their abilities, and treated with respect.

It turns out you can build a company that generates between $US50 million and US$70 million annually while being generous to workers. The Chicago-based software company Basecamp has done it. Its 54 employees work 40 hours a week at the most, and cut back to four standard days in summer, so everyone can enjoy a three-day weekend, but their pay stays the same. The list of employee benefits is mind-blowing: gym memberships and massages, subsidised co-working space rentals on request, US$,1000 a year each for continuing education and charitable donation matching, and heavily subsidised health-care premiums.

Exceptional in a US context (let alone by Silicon Valley standards) are the 16 weeks of maternity and six weeks of paternity leave, and a one-month paid sabbatical for every three years of service. Every employee can spend up to US$5,000 on an annual vacation, and Basecamp will cover it.

Not surprisingly, half of the employees – who are spread across multiple countries and mostly work on their own – have been with the company for more than five years. Everyone checks in through the Basecamp app to plan their work each morning and report back at the end of the day, and to share personal updates about weekends and family activities. Twice a year, the company flies all personnel into Chicago for a week.

Writing about Basecamp in *Lab Rats*, tech author Dan Lyons emphasises just how unusual Basecamp is for a company of its type. The founders like starting work at 9:30 in the morning, and 'don't want to be a three-hundred person company. We just wanted to build a company that we would want to work at.'

One founder, David Heinemeier Hansson, built a valuable web framework that he gives away for free as an open-source product; the other, Jason Fried, tells Lyons about the scornful tone of some Silicon Valley denizens: 'They tell us we're cute, we have a cute little lifestyle business ... Our people are happier. They spend time with their families ... People tell me, "Steve Jobs could not have made Apple if he took Fridays off." Well, I'm not trying to make Apple. And I don't care what Steve Jobs did.'

The work-life balance ingrained in the culture of Basecamp is supported by a simple productivity premise. Every employee should get eight hours of uninterrupted work time every day, and then their work day should end. Nobody needs eighty hours, Hansson says.

The Basecamp founders did not set out to run a thriving four-day week programme, but it has all the hallmarks of one. Technology is used to support collaboration and efficiency in work, while distractions are minimised. At the main office in Chicago, the enforcement of 'library rules' keeps noise down. Employees are given the tools and benefits to apply their full mental energy to their tasks. The leaders have cultivated a culture built on trust and open communication; they don't even track the hours each worker puts in.

Hansson and Fried are the antithesis of the plutocrats to whom Nick Hanauer issued his warning that 'pitchforks are coming' for them if they do not address rising inequality. They could be grabbing for the same brass ring as the household-name techpreneurs, but instead they have chased a different kind of exceptionalism. As Lyons writes:

These guys don't want to be the next Mark Zuckerberg ... They spend a lot of time encouraging aspiring entrepreneurs to pursue a healthier approach to operating a company. It starts with treating your employees well and looking after them. It also means looking after yourself. Work fewer hours. Avoid stress. Find happiness.[1]

FULLY FLEXED

Throughout this book I have talked about the four-day week in the context of flexibility policies, which can take dozens of forms within what are generally characterised as flexible work arrangements (FWAs).

Any deviation from the standard work week is considered an FWA. As the UC Davis article noted, the two main categories are flexibility on *where* the work is performed (e.g. at work or at home), and *when* the work is performed (e.g. during which hours and on which days). Another deviation is part-time work, i.e. regularly working less than 40 hours per week. Employees might want to work fewer hours to have time for other activities, such as family care or studying. Employers might want a more flexible workforce to increase the hours their company is available to its customers, or to increase the number of employees at work when demand peaks.

In the literature about flexible working arrangements in the developed world, FWAs can include everything from weekend work to shift work, overtime, annual-hours contracts, part-time work, job sharing, flexitime, temporary/casual work, fixed-term contracts, home-based work, teleworking and compressed working weeks. Until Perpetual Guardian's trial, there was no widely known example of a company reducing work hours while maintaining full-time pay that had been backed up by independent research.

The supporting theory of FWAs, based on international reports and studies of worker motivation and productivity, is that giving people more time to spend managing their personal responsibilities will energise them for their professional ones. There is mounting evidence that these mutually beneficial agreements between employers and employees (providing alternate options as to when, where and how much a person works) have measurable psychological, social and economic impacts.

Analysed on a raw cost basis, FWAs can reduce operating costs. Allowing people to work offsite some of the time cuts down on office space requirements and overheads. If an employee who has a sick child is permitted to work at home while caring for the child, they do not need to take leave to be away from the office.

The danger of inflexibility is that workers use leave in a piecemeal fashion to meet personal responsibilities, at the expense of a proper period of leave that gives them time to rest and recharge. FWAs mean the company can preserve the benefit of refreshed employees returning to work after annual leave.

Indeed, non-standard work patterns have been found to be related to decreased turnover in the private sector, while working outside the office was related to improved performance and reduced absenteeism. In general, absenteeism is less common in environments where managers are supportive of employees' need for flexibility, because employees have the capacity to work longer hours (on a flexible basis) before work-life conflict becomes problematic.

In the United States, Deloitte quantified its turnover-related cost savings due to the availability of FWAs at US$41.5 million in one year alone.[2] As it pertains to recruitment, a survey of 1,500 US workers found that nearly a third considered flexibility to be the *most* important aspect of an employment offer.[3] Additionally, 80 per cent of a cross-section of managers surveyed indicated that flexibility offerings impacted the recruitment of top talent.[4]

Satisfaction is a theme associated with flexibility, with Deloitte reporting that 84 per cent of clients are satisfied or very satisfied with the service provided by employees with FWAs, and only 1 per cent dissatisfied.

Likewise for workers themselves. JP Morgan Chase's annual employee survey found employees with an option of flexibility were much more likely to report overall satisfaction than those who felt they did not have access to flexibility.[5] New Zealand data on FWAs shows they aid employee outcomes like organisational commitment and job satisfaction – with the latter being the dominant predictor of job performance.[6]

There is evidence of a general receptiveness to the idea of flexibility as beneficial to a company. A study of the impact of Fortune 500 company profits in the *Wall Street Journal* found firms' stock prices rose an average 0.36 per cent following announcements of flexibility initiatives.[7] When looking at workplaces with established FWAs, researchers also found a positive association between the availability of FWAs (both remote working and schedule flexibility) and long-term financial performance.

A predicted boom in flexible working could contribute US$10.04 trillion to the global economy by 2030, according to the first comprehensive socio-economic study of changing workplace practices. New Zealand's share will be significant relative to the size and performance of its economy; between NZ$16.2 billion and NZ$18.1 billion is expected to be added, especially in several key industries, and between 74,000 and 83,000 additional jobs created. The analysis, commissioned by Regus (part of the IWG group of companies) and conducted by independent economists, studied 16 key countries to delve into the state of flexible working both now and through to 2030.[8]

Clearly you do not have to go far to make a case for FWAs on any grounds – economic, environmental or social and humane. People have more time to exercise, read, cook, catch up with friends, resume hobbies that fell by the wayside years ago. Our staff have told me it has changed their lives, and we can see in our data how much the needle has shifted in their reported health and job satisfaction.

Returning to social exchange theory, business leaders who have large numbers of staff on minimum or low wages should not underestimate the goodwill that will emanate – within and without the business – from a new work structure that immediately puts everyone on at least a living wage. Employees who are gifted a day off each week will be inclined, consciously or not, to exceed the agreed outputs, making the four-day week model potentially more productive than the five-day week. The value of giving people time to invest in themselves cannot be overstated.

PENSION HEADACHE

An extraordinary – and, I would argue, essential – advantage of the four-day week and other flexibility policies is their capacity to help refine the approach to superannuation, annual leave, sick leave and the minimum wage in the developed world, and in ways that can accommodate and even offset the pressures brought by the collision of aging populations with the Fourth Industrial Revolution. Without this refinement, the blithe, not-my-responsibility attitude of gig employers threatens to tear apart the intricate fabric of social protections that has accompanied organised labour for decades.

At the root of the looming budget crises in most developed nations is the rising burden of pension – also known as superannuation – and health costs, which are swelling as baby boomers enter retirement. Some countries, Australia being a notable example, have shown impressive foresight by establishing a compulsory-contribution pension system in which the quantum of the entitlement is linked to the accumulated monies in the pension pot.

Other nations (such as New Zealand, whose flirtation with compulsory retirement saving lasted a mere 37 weeks in the 1970s) are still grappling with legacy-defined benefits, where superannuation entitlements are related to annual salary and not to any contributions made to fund it.

For New Zealand, a liberal democracy with a large baby boomer population and a substantial social safety net, the daily superannuation cost is expected to rise from NZ$30 million at present to NZ$98 million in 20 years' time.[9] There is nothing in the national budget to meet this increase, which outstrips GDP growth and even the exploding rate of public health expenditure. A widespread four-day week would enable a portion of the work of caring for an aging population to be met within families, thus reducing the raw cost to the state. Otherwise, government and taxpayers will have to bear the full burden.

The voluntary, state-endorsed retirement scheme KiwiSaver, which started in 2007, cannot do much to offset this impact. For waged or salaried workers it pegs the default contribution rate at 3 per cent of gross salary (compared with the minimum of 9.5 per cent in Australia[10]), and until changes were introduced in April 2019, savers were permitted to take a 'contributions holiday' of up to five years. Around 135,000 New Zealanders are currently in this category.[11]

Clearly, a traditional, non-portable pension scheme does not work in an era of short-term contracts and people working multiple jobs. A straightforward realignment suited to twenty-first-century work models would have all temporary roles contributing to each worker's personal pension pot, with their pension reference being provided to everyone who gives that worker any form of employment, gig-based or otherwise. The reference would be a standard identifier already attached to that worker, such as a social security or tax number.

Using this as a basis, all employment contracts (including

the 'independent contracts' of the gig world) could require a defined percentage to be paid into an individual's pension pot by their employer. The Australian example proves this kind of compulsory defined contribution can, when phased in with proper notice, wash through the economy relatively quickly and without undue stress. The transition can happen smoothly when all employers are obligated to comply and the effect is felt, and absorbed, across all industries at once.

With this realignment, all workers, including those in the gig economy, have at least some personal provision for the future that cannot be arbitrated, circumvented or otherwise removed by the use of gig contracts. If the four-day week cannot, at least in the near future, become a widespread reality in developed economies, the financial futures of workers can and should be shored up by a fair and comprehensive approach to pension savings.

At the same time, as there is then a reduced incentive for employers to use gig from a cost perspective, there is consequently more pressure on employers to seek to offer flexibility within the structure of a conventional employment contract in order to meet the demand for flexible work from today's workers. I expect this will give impetus to the more widespread adoption of a four-day week.

LIVING THE DREAM

On the face of it, why should the Perpetual Guardian story mean anything at all? After all, we are 240 people out of the billions in the world. But we did this little experiment, and everything got brighter in our little corner of the planet. If you extrapolate our company's success beyond our walls and into the community, the potential is enormous.

We began to have an inkling of this on the day we announced the trial, when our staff were driving to meetings in branded cars and people were waving at them. Then the emails started coming in. Journalists wanted to know what we were up to. Business leaders and workers asked how we were doing it, and began the four-day week conversations in their own companies. After that, more people started engaging with us as potential clients of the business.

Start with our business and go wider. What if some of the biggest businesses in New Zealand, the employers of 1,000+ people, switched to a productivity focus and reduced the week to 32 hours based on delivery? If a big bank or telco did its homework, set the conditions and ran a trial that backed its workers on output, it would be a global sensation. From a cultural standpoint, it would completely change the game, and be the shove we so desperately need to move the world of work into a twenty-first-century model which meets economic and human needs on an equal basis.

The four-day week would give people a time advantage that sets them up to succeed in a shifting world. Rather than fearing their job will become obsolete or their industry will be taken over by artificial intelligence, they can use the extra time to retrain and learn new skills. Perhaps most importantly, it could make inroads into the epidemic afflicting workers all over the world. In New Zealand, one in five people in the workforce at any time has depression, anxiety, panic disorder or another mental health condition. As the UK data shows, work-related stress is a major cause of and exacerbating factor in mental ill-health.[12]

The energy and airspace already given to the four-day week is proof of the need for it. From the companies around the world that have reached out in curiosity and endorsement, to the request from the Australian government for advice to its public services, to the UK unions which have explicitly named the four-day week as aspirational – the momentum is building towards legislative change which breaks the old, rigid mould of the five-day 9 to 5.

From my vantage point at the bottom of the world, I can see the pendulum shifting around the globe, as the thinking begins to change at the highest levels of business and government. When I want to remind myself of the real meaning of the four-day week, I think of the dad who got to pick up his child from school for the first time ever; of the single mum who saved hundreds of dollars on childcare and was able to spend more time with her son; and of the lovely young couple who decided to have a baby.

IN BRIEF

- The example of the American software company Basecamp proves significant market capitalisation and multimillion-dollar annual turnover can go hand-in-glove with generous provisions, including flexibility, for workers.

- There is mounting evidence that flexible working arrangements, as mutually beneficial agreements between employers and employees (providing alternate options as to when, where and how much a person works), have measurable psychological, social and economic impacts – from a reduction in company operating costs to enhanced client and employee satisfaction.

- Long-term pension savings are endangered by a gig-economy model which circumvents the established rights of workers; a four-day week can offset this risk while offering flexibility alongside standard worker protections, as can a realignment of legislation to ensure that all employers and workers, gig or otherwise, can be supported to make steady contributions for retirement.

- The four-day week is a model of work which can meet the human and economic needs of the modern developed world equally, setting people up to succeed in work and in the rest of their lives.

CHAPTER NINE

The Obstacles

THE RIGHT SIDE OF THE LAW

In designing the four-day week, we were forced to think creatively. Imagination with a side of legal advice was about the only way we could overcome the inadequacy of the Employment Relations Act 2000, the current legislation governing how people work in New Zealand. Specifically, we had to align our programme to comply with section 67C, which is prescriptive as to normal working hours, start and finish times, the days of the week designated for work, and – in a surprising outbreak of legalistic flair – 'any flexibility' in the matters aforementioned.[1]

Upon close examination, this tantalising reference proved misleading; in practice, the Act's approach to working hours did not facilitate the easy adoption of a flexible working hours programme. I suspect this is the case with most employment legislation globally, which is based on hours 'worked' rather than productivity.

Our creative solution was the opt-in model. This requires the employee to actively choose the four-day week – it cannot be forced upon them – and invest the company with the power to withdraw the 'gift' if the employee does not hold up their side of the bargain.

This model – the gift and the potential for withdrawal if the employee does not deliver the agreed productivity outcomes – cements a general understanding that changes in behaviour and process must be introduced and maintained if the programme is to succeed, and employees have both a right and a responsibility to draw attention to any factor outside their control undermining their ability to meet their part of the agreement.

Here is the primary external obstacle to widespread adoption of the four-day week by business leaders: nowhere in the world is such a model explicitly mandated, or even provided for, in any employment legislation. We had no precedent to follow in proposing a long-term four-day week at Perpetual Guardian, and we had to ensure that by doing the right thing by our staff, who had collectively proved the validity of the four-day week in the trial phase, we were not inadvertently falling foul of the law.

Enter two leading New Zealand law firms. We asked each one for a legal opinion on our intended productivity policy. In particular, we sought to understand how the company could reserve the right to remove the 'productivity week', as we referred internally to our four-day week policy, without repercussion.

In a summary of its legal opinion, one firm said:

Perpetual Guardian can retain flexibility [in its right to withdraw the four-day week opt-in model] by ensuring guiding documents are clear in retaining discretion, managing representations made during recruitment, monitoring practices to avoid unhelpful patterns emerging, and justifying any decision to remove the policy.

The onus was on our leadership to ensure the policy did not, by default, become the de facto terms of employment for our staff, which we could not undo.

This was critical, as intrinsic to the four-day week model is the right of its 'owner' – the company decision-maker/s – to remove or withdraw the policy at any time, based on a failure to meet the conditions agreed with individual workers. In offering the 'gift' of the four-day week to staff who choose to take it and who consistently comply with the terms, we had to ensure the policy did not form part of our employment agreements.

It might sound counter-intuitive, but the only way we could make the four-day week function within the confines of current New Zealand legislation was by leaving the terms and conditions of employment unchanged, including remuneration, and by preserving the official hours of work under the standard full-time model.

In leaving the individual employment agreements unchanged from the previous five-day week, we could ensure employees would continue to accrue all leave and other entitlements at the normal – that is, full-time – rate. Those employees who chose the four-day week signed an opt-in form which stated their and the company's obligations under the new, long-term model.

From the perspective of the company's leaders and directors, our approach to the legal and contractual issues was a leap, but an informed one. We had insulated ourselves from legal risk by designing a new opt-in programme which complemented but did not alter or override existing employment contracts, and we had left ourselves an 'out' in case the long-term productivity week did not work as well as the trial had.

The downside of this approach was that the core terms of the contracts had not changed – we were obliged to accrue leave on the basis of a 'normal' five-day week. In effect, we were accruing four days' leave on the 40 or so extra days a year we were gifting our staff.

This is, of course, an example of how the rigidity of employment legislation restricts the ability of businesses to attempt to provide better flexibility – and in our case, even penalises them for attempting it!

At the time of writing, legislators in the developed world are not acting overtly to facilitate new models of work such as the four-day week. Most companies which choose to replicate our course of action will likely need to follow a comparable process for their own legal protection and to ring-fence the existing rights of their workers.

There should be little surprise legislators are not reacting in a timely fashion to the needs of the modern workplace. The failure of legislators to act as many tech companies ride roughshod over existing regulations indicates most legislators haven't yet recognised the necessity for more active intervention to protect the rights of workers. As was the case in earlier industrial eras, the companies most cavalier about the rules of work are those reinventing it, with tech titans being enthusiastic exploiters of the gig – the ultimate incarnation of the current epoch's fusion of labour and digitalisation.

However, there are some signs of a mounting defence against *in*flexibility and poor work-life balance, such as The Schedules That Work Act of 2017 in the United States, which protects workers who request schedule changes and those in industries known for unstable and unpredictable scheduling;[2] and the agreement in 2018 between Germany's largest trade union, IG Metall, and a large employers' group to introduce an optional 28-hour working week for 900,000 workers in the metals and electrical industries.[3]

The complaint about IG Metall's 'win' for workers is that it places a burden on businesses that will be hard to bear, especially given the possibility this 28-hour week, a 20 per cent reduction from the standard 35, will extend over time to other industries. If so, its difference from the Perpetual Guardian model will be more widely felt; while the IG Metall members who choose the reduced working week may be rewarded with better work-life balance, they will only be paid for the hours worked.

It is safe to assume the union and industrial employers have hedged their bets on the productivity effects of a shorter week by reducing compensation for it, and by agreeing the shorter week will only be offered for up to two years, after which workers must return to 35 hours.[4] While these industries, and the German economy in general, do continue to deliver enviably high rates of productivity, this is likely attributable to higher past investment in technology rather than a current improvement in the actual output of individual workers.

Indeed, we should question whether there is evidence any reduced work-week policy, whether legislated or negotiated, is effective in increasing either productivity or engagement if it is not conditional upon these improvements. Without explicit conditions, what is to stop prevailing work habits and patterns which inhibit output continuing unchecked? There is little benefit to a company if a shorter work week still includes institutionalised inefficiency and hours a day of social media surfing, overlong meetings and other unproductive activity. In such circumstances, it is all but inevitable output will fall and the policy will be abandoned.

Workers' rights, as they have evolved from the First Industrial Revolution to today, have never included specific provisions for flexibility. If a company wants to offer it, in most jurisdictional contexts it must go through complex and often costly contortions to find a legal way to 'gift' any time off that is not mandated or allowed in employment legislation.

Which is an interesting thought: for all the time we spend thinking about and advocating for the rights of workers, what about the rights of company owners and leaders to set flexible employment terms that are more compassionate, and better overall for the company and its employees, but beyond the initiative of the law?

FREE YOUR LOCAL WAGE SLAVE

It has always struck me as ironic that people condemn products made using child labour or extremely low-paid workers, yet when it comes to grabbing a convenient takeaway or ride, the same people value convenience and cost over the rights of their compatriots. Wage slavery comes in many forms, and even if there are no literal chains or whips in sight, today's most unprotected workers can nonetheless find themselves in shackles.

Gig working is a trap from which workers struggle to break free, in large part because it is hard to build financial momentum and because opportunities to upskill and uptrain, and thus progress in a career, are not readily available. The four-day week, conversely, offers all the expected advantages of permanent employment, including the opportunity for professional development and further education, in addition to the flexibility that is the chief selling point of the gig.

There is mounting evidence this gig trap is growing larger and swallowing more of the workforce, particularly younger people and newer migrants who may not have a work history in their adopted country. But freeing wage slaves starts with examining what governs work; that is, the employers who are dutifully obeying traditional employment legislation.

Likewise, the four-day week can only become a pillar in the future of work if legislators modify existing laws to be adaptable to a variety of flexibility policies, which may be desirable to the many employers who see the potential rewards in shorter work weeks with a more intense focus on output.

In short, if we are to create appropriate freedoms in work while shoring up the responsibilities shouldered by workers and employers alike, the existing legislative models must change comprehensively, country by country.

The primary objective of employment legislation should be to set out principles rather than prescriptions, and to create space for employers and employees to agree on flexible terms that benefit both parties. Detractors of a four-day week or other flexible work models might suggest that provisions for flexibility weaken employment legislation, but this is a false argument, and indeed a circular one. In practice, the current prescriptive tone of much legislation undermines the economy and workforce by creating an opportunity for employers and companies to circumvent its provisions, but stay within the law, by using gig contracts.

I contend that, once the appropriate loadings for pension savings and annual and sick leave are added to all contracts, and minimum wage protections are embedded, the temptation for employers to contract out of employment legislation will be reduced. There will be no avenue for workers to be left unprotected, and all employers will share equal responsibility for protecting their workforce. Companies will have more leeway to come to mutually advantageous terms with workers, and no business will bear an unfair burden while others skate merrily around the perimeter of the law.

We can create a framework which permits the maximum amount of flexibility while ensuring basic and hard-won protections for the social good remain in force for all the

workforce. There should be no debate over whether governments have a duty of care for their citizens. People must be
given an opportunity to earn at a level that delivers a minimum standard of quality of life, and provides sufficiently for
retirement, illness and injury, so there is not undue financial pressure on either individuals or companies, now or in
the future.

Many governments, past and present, are guilty of kicking
the can down the road on all kinds of issues, because the solution is complicated or expensive or simply a hard sell to the
electorate. No political leader should be allowed by voters to
overlook any endangerment of workers' rights, if only because
the future fiscal burden of failing to ensure our citizens have
appropriate financial safeguards in the form of pension and
sickness benefits will be borne by all taxpayers.

Those most affected will be the millennial and Gen Z
cohorts, the very generations which have seen traditional
employment contracts replaced by the independent gig model.
If they had any hope of accruing personal assets comparable
with those held by baby boomers, the wealthiest generation
in history, it is being killed by the refashioning of the rules of
employment by powerful gig owners.

How can we fix typical employment legislation to ring-
fence rights while permitting flexibility? First, the law should
not be overly prescriptive as to normal start and finish times
or to what constitutes a 'normal' work week. In modern,
pluralistic societies, the sanctity of Sunday as a day of rest has
diminished, and there is a valid argument that while legislation might define a normal working week (say, five days from
8.30 a.m. to 5 p.m.), people should be free to choose to work
outside those times.

In practice, in settings not unionised or subject to central bargaining arrangements, companies can circumvent

provisions for working hours by using contracts to avoid, for example, weekend loading. Therefore, why not permit people to opt in to work non-standard hours within the statutory protections for the length of the work day and work week?

On this basis, workers in a gig economy can choose when and where they work without forgoing the rightful benefits of employment. Contracts with defined working times, including weekends, could be offered, but if not enough workers opt in, further financial inducements such as loading may be needed. The employer will need to give a little more to get more – the most likely real-world outcome of a flexibility clause in employment legislation is a gentle push-pull between negotiators that does not place too much power in the hands of any one party.

The upshot is employers and employees should be free to implement flexible working conditions that are fairer and more beneficial than the minimums set out in legislation. If we genuinely seek to address economic productivity and the social issues associated with how we work, the first priority for amendment should be to make basic terms, such as start and finish times and the duration of the work week (subject to a maximum number of hours in a week), adjustable by agreement.

If we fail to make our employment legislation fit for purpose, the gig economy will grow unchecked, and I predict more companies which rely on traditional employment agreements will be seduced by the hazy promise of 'Agile' contract-based strategies. Gig by another name, the Agile craze has little apparent social benefit and, if applied widely and with faddish enthusiasm by misguided CEOs and HR directors, threatens to weaken and dismantle the very employee protections that a four-day week is designed to strengthen.

CONSUMER CONSCIENCE

Governments everywhere are faced with the problem of how to balance the need for welcoming the technology-based businesses of the twenty-first century, and at the same time recognising those companies unchained by lax or outdated regulation or legislation (or by the outlaw mentality of a start-up) are creating social and economic challenges. This book explores the role of the four-day week in influencing change for the better in corporate and employment practices, but I would be remiss if I let consumers off the hook. They too have a critical part to play in ensuring the future of employment works for the many, not just the few.

As users of products and services, we share a collective responsibility to assess whether the companies we patronise are operating ethically, and to judge them on how they behave towards their employees or contractors, their communities and the environment. Earlier in this book, I argued convenience is the twenty-first-century opium of the people – so how many of our purchasing decisions are driven by a desire for the lowest price and immediate gratification? How often do our better angels win, and we opt for the higher price or slower delivery in the interests of the environment or our fellow humans?

We have discussed how convenience appears to trump all other considerations among consumers. Is a similar ethos – do whatever is most convenient, no matter the consequences – becoming the new philosophy of the corporate world? If we consider some of the biggest corporate ethics stories of the past few years, from the Volkswagen emissions scandal to money laundering at Danske and Facebook's litany of problems, including data breaches and alleged complicity in election interference, it's awfully hard to resist cynicism.

We are told companies need to operate ethically to safe-guard their viability. The assumption is consumers demand good behaviour and will boycott businesses if they don't approve of their conduct. But the evidence suggests otherwise. People still buy VWs, and #DeleteFacebook has not become a medium-obliterating trend.

Of course, these are generalisations. Consumer boycotts have long been used to considerable effect, and there are many examples of companies doing the right thing and seeking constantly to improve. The challenge to us all – responsible businesspeople, consumers, policymakers and anyone with influence in a boardroom – is to use whatever power we wield for good.

We are at a considerable advantage in that it has never been more difficult for companies to conceal poor practices. For instance, the *Telegraph*'s analysis of the real cost to society of extremely inexpensive fast fashion highlighted the UK-based online retailer Boohoo, which admitted selling £5 dresses as a loss leader to entice consumers to explore the site further and buy the slightly pricier, profitable items.[5]

The loss leader has been a core feature of retail practice for decades, but the web has rewritten the old rules of commerce. Now, when buyers race to snap up clothing that costs next to nothing, high-street stores and bricks-and-mortar retail chains can't compete, as a wave of store closures by Marks and Spencer, Toys R Us, Walmart, Starbucks and Gap, among many others, has proved. The microeconomic effects are equally punitive, in that the people who make those cheap clothes are often earning less than a living wage – and they are not all in developing countries.

A *Financial Times* investigation found that part of the garment industry in Leicester, in England's industrial heartland, historically a stronghold of the rag trade, 'has become detached from UK employment law, "a country within a country", as one factory owner puts it, where "£5 an hour is considered the top wage", even though that is illegal'.[6] The UK has a mandated minimum wage for over-25s of £7.83 an hour, and when questioned by the *Telegraph*, a Leicester-based factory pointed to non-enforcement of various employment laws by way of explanation.[7]

In short, they are complying with the demands of high street and online fast fashion retailers (all operating in a competitive, if not cut-throat, market) at the expense of the law, while authorities turn a blind eye to a stream of labour exploitation.[8*] If regulators are not scrupulous about monitoring and enforcement, some company owners will seize the opportunity to ride roughshod over people – and when this is taken to its natural conclusion, with many powers colluding in an amoral approach to business, you get outcomes like the global financial crisis.

It is not absurd to view the gig model of work as another example of millions of people being experimented on economically by a relative handful of corporations and leaders – or to see, as I do, the four-day week as one way to bring business back into line and restore the balance of power between corporation and worker in a way that does not require businesses to sacrifice productivity or profitability.

I suspect, based on the data, directors and CEOs of large corporates have realised the shelf life of a bad news story is

---

* Perhaps the strangest thing about this labour exploitation is that it is an open secret. Central government knows; local government knows; retailers know. 'When I came to the UK and I discovered what was going on in Leicester, it was mind-blowing,' says Anders Kristiansen, who was chief executive of high-street retailer New Look from 2013 until September last year. 'This is happening in front of your eyes and nobody's doing anything?!' he remembers thinking. 'How can society accept it – not even society, how can government accept it? It's so sad, I've not spoken about it for a long time because it frustrated me so much.'

so brief they can generally get away with the mistake or the deception as long as they show no sign of weakness. Bolstering this attitude is the fact targeted news feeds and filters mean very few issues gain the notice of consumers, and if a given story doesn't reach a wide audience on social platforms, it might barely resonate.

If there is little rigour among many consumers in evaluating the labour or environmental costs of operators, others are becoming more mindful, and entrepreneurs are spying a main chance. Sara Arnold, the founder of UK-based fashion rental company Higher Studio, told the *Telegraph* her business empowered its customers to 'enjoy fashion without worrying about the environmental impact' because the model lets people avoid abetting the crimes of fast fashion by renting their wardrobes instead.[9]

It's far from a perfect concept, from a sustainability standpoint – items are delivered and collected by next-day courier, and everything is dry-cleaned between rentals – but at least the very demand for environmental awareness in fashion represents a shift in the industry, albeit a relatively recent one. When Arnold graduated from Central Saint Martins in 2012, 'the topic of sustainability was only an obligatory concern during my undergraduate course in Fashion Design and Marketing – it had almost no demand from my fellow students. An active minority of us felt like outsiders.'

Now, she says, 'an ecosystem of idealistic sustainable practices and research is ... cultivated in universities', and she cites as proof a 2018 Boston Consulting Group report which found 75 per cent of fashion companies improved their sustainability score in 2017, compared with 2016.[10] It is precisely this kind of thinking which supports a four-day week or other flexible working model that ring-fences the rights of workers. Sara Arnold may describe these sustainable practices as idealistic, but they are increasingly an everyday reality for many companies.

A helpful gauge for consumers which has grown in recent years is the B Lab, an organisation for social good in business which certifies companies as B Corporations based on an assessment of a company's impact on its workers, customers, community and environment. Certified B Corporations, or B Corps, now number 2,500+ in more than 50 countries, and include Patagonia, Natura and Danone.

Recognising '[s]ociety's most challenging problems cannot be solved by government and nonprofits alone', the B Lab and Certified B Corporations, or B Corps, 'are accelerating a global culture shift to redefine success in business and build a more inclusive and sustainable economy.'[11]

This includes, the organisation says, promoting the highest standards of public transparency and legal accountability – which, as we have canvassed, is not the strong suit of all business and industries, and we can hardly blame consumers for not always being able to distinguish the honest operators from the rest.

Perhaps the moral imperative for purchasing decisions is they are informed by the adage about something being too good to be true: when you buy that improbably cheap consumer item, someone else is paying the price you won't. It might be the children of the Leicester textile worker who are going without, because how do you house and raise a family on £40 a day?

This is a problem of inequality we can solve, if we start advocating for ourselves and each other. My argument for a four-day week is part of that advocacy, and a bid to forestall any more unnecessary crises of financial systems which trickle down to cause hardship to millions of people. The case for a four-day week is one of productivity, profitability and worker well-being – but it is also an impassioned call for sound ethics in business, and a vision that is entirely within reach.

IN BRIEF

- The opt-in model treats the four-day week as an employee 'gift' which may be withdrawn if the employee does not deliver the agreed productivity outcomes.

- Changes to employment legislation will make the four-day week and other flexible work models viable across countries and economies. New or updated legislation should set out principles rather than prescriptions and create space for employers and employees to agree on flexible terms that benefit both parties.

- The four-day week can only become a pillar in the future of work if legislators modify existing laws to be adaptable to a variety of flexibility policies, which may be desirable to the many employers who see the potential rewards in shorter work weeks with a more intense focus on output.

- The most likely real-world outcome of a flexibility clause in employment legislation is a gentle push-pull between negotiators that does not place too much power in the hands of any one party.

- We share a collective responsibility to assess whether the companies we patronise are operating ethically, and to judge them on how they behave towards their employees or contractors, their communities and the environment.

- The four-day week is both an argument for and a manifestation of ethical business operations; as industries continue to move towards more sustainable models, the question of sustainable employment – that which supports physical, mental and financial well-being and rebuffs the hand-to-mouth nature of the gig – becomes paramount.

CHAPTER TEN

Inside the Business Walls

Over the past year I have travelled to some of the biggest business hubs on the planet, talking about the four-day week and the future of work with founders, CEOs, philanthropists and entrepreneurs. To a person, they are inquisitive and open-minded, curious to learn how we have changed our business model to focus on productivity, not time. But I have encountered a considerable amount of intellectual resistance when the idea is mooted for their own organisations. Many leaders have congratulated me with enthusiasm and explained why they think the four-day week is terrific, but it would never work in their business.

This resistance – whether it stems from doubt, fear or genuine scepticism that a 'productivity time' equation can maintain profitability and keep shareholders happy – is the biggest internal obstacle to the four-day week. It is the reason why some of the biggest companies will be the slowest adopters. The banks, insurers and telcos will erroneously perceive a threat to their bottom lines and will start to consider meaningful flexibility and productivity policies only when they begin to lose the talent war, and when the rate of staff sickness and burnout becomes too high to support.

The views espoused by some entrepreneurs, that ultra-long work weeks are a 'huge blessing' (Jack Ma)[1] and necessary to 'change the world' (Elon Musk)[2], only perpetuate the myth that long hours lead to increases in productivity and profitability. What Ma and Musk both seem not to grasp is few employees can match them for stamina or appetite for work, or would want to even if they could.

Sacrificing such things as rest, family time, community connection and social activity in order to work is commonly known as workaholism, and we have more data than ever showing the toxicity of overwork to the human body. Working '996' (9 a.m. to 9 p.m., six days a week), as Ma has called for among the Chinese workforce, or 80 to 100 hours a week, as Musk recommends, is likely to increase the risk of a host of health complications, from Type 2 diabetes to some cancers and cognitive disorders such as dementia.[3]

For those whose jobs are primarily sedentary, the recent study of 8,000 workers by Columbia University Medical Center was alarming in its finding that sitting in an office for long periods has a similar physiological effect to smoking.[4]

Furthermore, there is no credible evidence to suggest the more you work, the more productive, creative and efficient you become – in fact, the opposite is true.[5] More than anything, Ma's and Musk's remarks evince a surprisingly nineteenth-century attitude, more reflective of the dark satanic mills of old England than the bright offices of complex modern industry.

A comparable analogy to the four-day week resistance among some prominent founders and business leaders is of print media owners who were looking the wrong way when the internet began to encroach on their territory. Countless millions in potential revenue were lost, titles were shuttered and traditional journalism was all but decimated. The visionaries and founders who understood how to harness the power of digital media – for better and for worse – have never looked back.

We are approaching a similar tipping point in the future of work. Companies in many industries and countries are experimenting with flexibility policies and tiptoeing up to the hard line of a four-day week trial. In my conversations with some of them, I am being reminded that a productivity policy is primarily a test of leadership. The ability of the leader to comprehend the potential application of the policy in their business, and then articulate it to staff and other decision-makers, will seal its fate.

Having become something of an informal four-day week consultant, I can observe this trend up close. In Chapter Six I referred to a UK entity whose policy director contacted me to say he was interested in our 'revolutionary' idea, and as we developed the four-day week policy at Perpetual Guardian over the course of 2018, I stayed in touch with him. We met in person in early 2019 to discuss the viability of the four-day week for the foundation – just as the director was about to make a case to his board recommending every staff member should have Friday off.

I explained to the director the whole organisation shutting its doors for a full day every week ran counter to the principles of the productivity policy, which is based in part on the maintenance of standard customer service levels. I felt the proposal as it stood was unlikely to find favour with his board, and emailed him with my other recommended 'rules' to make the four-day week work.

He later emailed back to advise the entity had decided against implementing the four-day week; there was not enough internal support.

It is an enlightening example of that first roadblock, resistance at the decision-making level. The policy director does not say whether there is fervent internal opposition to a trial, or whether the problem is a milder one of general reluctance to be the person who issues the final authorisation and can therefore be held accountable if it doesn't work out. Either way, it amounts to the same thing – maintenance of the status quo. No one makes a move, and the staff are destined to remain in the world of work as it is today.

This example also reveals a second common obstacle, which is a misconception of the definition of 'four-day week'. If mistranslated as 'three-day weekend', successful adoption is not impossible, but it is much more difficult if there is any expectation the organisation will maintain consistent communication and service to a market over a standard week. Many companies do not even close down on weekends, and few CEOs or boards can be expected to countenance a four-day week in which most or all staff are absent on the same day.

Finally, in my conversations with founders and CEOs I am emphatic about office design as a potential internal roadblock to optimal organisational health; specifically, that open-plan offices are the enemy of productivity.

If people are at desks or cubicles in close proximity and within earshot, and there are no rules governing when they can interrupt each other, output will suffer. When a worker is concentrating on a complex task and is disturbed, it will take them approximately 40 minutes to reach the level of productivity and focus they had at the time they were interrupted. A study by the Institute of Psychiatry in London found persistent interruptions at work caused a 10-point drop in the IQ of the person being distracted – twice the decline found in studies of the impact of marijuana use.[6,7]

When I first read about the UK and Canadian workplace productivity studies, I wondered about the impediments. Why are people going to work, but not actually working? We can roughly break it down by social, organisational and personal factors. As multiple studies have found, a typical day for many workers includes a chat with colleagues, a cup of coffee, a quick surf of news sites, checking some emails, having a meeting, making a personal phone call ... and this ritual can be repeated several times in a given day.

It is not deliberate time-wasting, but it reflects how we have designed our workspaces. Fewer people are shutting themselves away in an office or working on a production line; work involves a lot of interaction and unstructured social time. This can be a boon for workplace morale, but unless the socialisation is oriented towards a goal (e.g. a lunchtime walking meeting), it is absurd to expect consistently high productivity. As we saw earlier, one UK survey found that we have built little distractions like social media into our work lives; 79 per cent of respondents admitted they weren't productive for the entire time they were at work, and 54 per cent reported looking forward to the distractions which made their working day more bearable.[8]

As covered in Chapter Six, the success of the four-day week trial will rest partly on the willingness of staff in an open-plan environment to collaborate on a low-noise, no-interruption plan. A strategy designed for maximum productivity is likely to involve both technological and refreshingly old-school solutions (the Do Not Disturb smartphone function and the flag in the pencil pot), and may even prompt the healthy airing of workplace-behaviour grievances that have been festering for some time. The latter is probably nothing for HR to fret about; when everyone has their eyes on a collective prize, there is little room for conflict.

The big-ticket obstacles to fundamental change in how we work are likely to be broken down incrementally, through a combination of organised labour activity and a growing body of evidence that shows there is a better way to work and live. I would not underestimate the role of climate change activism by millennials and Gen Z in reducing carbon emissions from traffic congestion and, by extension, creating productivity-enhancing flexibility in when and where vast numbers of people go to work.

When they are 'at work', may they be so lucky as to be led by people who are willing to consider valid data, challenge existing precepts and experiment with new business practices that can *really* change the world.

IN BRIEF

- Intellectual resistance among company leaders is the biggest internal obstacle to the four-day week.

- The views espoused by entrepreneurs such as Jack Ma and Elon Musk only perpetuate the myth that long hours lead to increases in productivity and profitability. There is no credible evidence to suggest the more you work, the more productive, creative and efficient you become – in fact, the opposite is true.

- A flexibility or productivity policy is primarily a test of leadership. The ability of the leader to comprehend the potential application of the policy in their business, and then articulate it to staff and other decision-makers, will seal its fate.

- A common obstacle is the mistranslation of 'four-day week' as 'three-day weekend'. In such cases successful adoption is not impossible, but it is much more difficult if there is any expectation the organisation will maintain consistent communication and service to a market over a standard week.

- Data shows that open-plan offices are the enemy of productivity. They can foster a lot of interaction and unstructured social time which make it absurd to expect consistently high productivity.

- The success of a four-day week trial will rest partly on the willingness of staff in an open-plan environment to collaborate on a low-noise, no-interruption plan.

Cows Need Milking Twice a Day

During the New Zealand autumn of 2019 I visited Wellington, the country's centre of government, to discuss the four-day week with a Member of Parliament. On the waiting room couch I was joined by someone who was there to see another MP.

We exchanged pleasantries, and he enquired about the reason for my visit. When I explained the productivity week concept, he gave me a sceptical look and asked, 'Do you think it's applicable to every business?'

'Yes,' I said.

He leaned back on the couch and was silent. After about a minute, he turned to me again. 'Well, how would it work in dairy? After all, cows need milking twice a day!'

I was nonplussed, having never much considered the daily routines of cattle, but I recognised this response for what it was. Instinctively, he had searched his mind for proof the concept is flawed; the one thing that shows it can't work. To the sceptic, the four-day week is provocative, even bizarre.

Naturally, they draw on their own experience and preconceptions to form an argument against it.

But let's return to the example of dairy, to which change has already come. A hundred years ago, we had smaller herds, with more farmhands to feed, milk and care for the animals. As industrialised farming developed through the twentieth century, milking equipment was mechanised and vehicles and other machinery grew more sophisticated and efficient, so herd sizes grew but the complement of farm workers shrank. With scientific advances, feed and husbandry have improved and milk yields have risen accordingly.

Now we are in an age of full automation and constant reinvention, with apps and drone-based technology refining farming protocols, pioneering concepts such as A2 milk raising the bar on yields and profits, and the demand for labour declining still further.

All this means higher output on a per-capita basis, so there is no reason why the operations of an efficient, highly automated farm could not adapt to a shift-based four-day week which maintains profitability and improves the quality of life of those on the land.

I have to pose these questions to the sceptics: Why, after years of advancements in technology and process, would innovation cease now? Does the five-day week, the 9 to 5, the relentless slog through rush hour represent the pinnacle of everyday commercial endeavour? Is there nothing we can do better?

Oddly enough, we may have been unintentionally doing the right thing all along. In the study of work, an oft-referenced prediction is that of John Maynard Keynes, who said in 1930 that with the rise of automation, humans would work only 15 hours per week.[1] On the face of it, he was way off-base, not least because he could scarcely have foreseen the spillage, mostly through digital connectivity, of working hours into private life. Many experts predicted a bountiful leisure dividend from accessible and inexpensive technology. Quite the opposite, at least in most industries in developed countries, has been delivered.

Look closer, though, and was Keynes wrong? He was thinking about productivity when he made his prediction, which itself came in a time when measurements of output were easier to access given most countries had a predominantly industrial base.

Perhaps Keynes would be unsurprised to learn of the two studies which catalysed the four-day week story – the UK and Canadian researchers who attempted to determine the actual output of office workers. Remember, the estimated productive time was between 1.5 and 2.5 hours a day, and according to another study a loftier (but still low) 2 hours and 53 minutes – making for a true work week of around 14.5 hours maximum.

On the evidence that the rest of the time spent at work is largely 'filler' – drawn-out meetings, personal calls, social media browsing and break-room chats – it looks like Keynes was on to something. The data shows that productive work is coalescing at almost exactly the level he predicted, and most hours 'at work' are in the mode of leisure, busywork and general time-wasting to meet the standard 40 (or more) hours expected by employers.

The 15-hour phenomenon is not surprising given the failure of the construct of the working week to keep pace with the changing impact of technology on work. In previous industrial eras, work comprised mostly of physical labour and craftsmanship; today's worker is more than likely doing tasks using a computer or mobile device. Scrupulous attention to productive tasks is difficult to maintain, and output is harder to measure than it would have been for, say, a coal miner. This very mode of work, coupled with the constant interferences and inter-ruptions of tech devices and busy workplaces, encourages distractions and impedes productivity.

On a broader scale, changing family structures, the length-ening of commutes and the intrusion of work into home life mean that communities are not as well formed or collectively supportive as in the past. As an employer, I theorise this is causing many of today's workers to experience their place of work as a primary source of social interaction.

Meanwhile, Keynes could not have known how con-sumption would grow – how we would become mass over-consumers, demanding more and more goods even at the expense of our health and the viability of human life on Earth. At the heart of the work problem may be consumption levels and associated waste; the funds needed to buy consumer prod-ucts and the human labour needed to make them are driving longer work hours and the deleterious environmental effects of all that activity.

If that is true, would we be willing to accept a decline in consumption levels in exchange for a radical reduction in work hours if it meant better quality of human life and enduring climate security?

Let's look at the biggest picture of all.

In his latest book, *Upheaval: Turning Points for Nations in Crisis,* the geography professor, historian and science writer Jared Diamond sets a deadline. If we have not, as complex, globalised societies, figured out a sustainable use of resources by about 2050, the world as we know it will end. More than that, he says we have four specific problems to solve as an international community if humanity is to endure: the risk of nuclear holocaust, climate change, unsustainable resource use and inequality.[2]

Even if Diamond is only partly right, it is a sobering picture.

In the 18 months or so since I conceived the four-day week, it has become apparent that as a global community we must reappraise everything about how we live if we are to address serious public health issues such as work-related stress and mental illness, and to begin the task of rebalancing the distribution of wealth.

From the French Revolution to the Great Depression and World War II, and countless more examples besides, we have incontrovertible proof that a stable world order and the general well-being of human populations depends on the maintenance of certain expectations. In developed nations, we have come to expect that work is widely available and provides sufficient income for people to house and feed their families, educate their children and access good healthcare. When those expectations are subverted or unmet for large numbers of people, the political and social order is destabilised and the results can be catastrophic.

In *The 4 Day Week*, I have argued for and demonstrated the value of a productivity-focused, reduced-hour model of work for companies and industries. I have examined the risks presented by an unfettered gig economy and sounded a warning about the vulnerability of hard-won worker protections. Now is the time to make the connection between how we work and the crises of individual and planetary suffering.

No one doubts we are in a new industrial era whose economic ramifications are all but impossible to predict; no one is avowing that human well-being, especially as it pertains to our work lives, is optimal. What we now know is that a tentative or piecemeal approach is unlikely to be enough to meet the threats we face; if we need radical action on climate change, we must be just as radical in changing how we work.

Oddly enough, our crisis is the product of our success as a species. We have been so productive and reproductive, staving off mortality and converting resources in service of our own propagation, that we now have to rethink, in some extreme and immediate ways, how we can stop ourselves becoming casualties of our own pre-eminence. If we do not, something is going to give, whether it is Earth's capacity to support us, the global order, or another, unforeseen thing.

At least governments and citizens are finally comprehending en masse the scale of our planetary predicament. From the 1960s, when Rachel Carson's writing catalysed the modern environmental movement, to the mid-2000s, as Al Gore's crusade added political weight to the cause, scientists have reached a consensus and denial has become a lowly populated province.

No longer a pet policy, climate change promises to be a central issue in the 2020 US presidential election. The Trump administration's withdrawal from the Paris Agreement, far from stymying progress, has arguably accelerated the movement for a truly global compact to save Earth and its species – one in which American state governors, mayors and CEOs have coalesced to compensate for the inaction of the federal government.[3] Forget MAGA – this rebel coalition wants to Make Earth Thrive Again.

At last, we have collectively realised the baton of responsibility for the climate cannot be passed to the next generation, because there will be no one there to take it.

As I was writing this book, two climate reports landed like grenades. In 2018, the International Panel on Climate Change issued a Special Report which predicted, with high confidence, global warming of 1.5°C above pre-industrial levels by between 2030 and 2052 at the current rate. The consequence, the panel said, would be increased climate-related 'risks to health, livelihoods, food security, water supply, human security and economic growth.'[4]

The report further noted that '[p]athways limiting global warming to 1.5°C ... would require rapid and far-reaching transitions in energy, land, urban and infrastructure (including transport and buildings), and industrial systems'.

Then, in May 2019, came the IPBES Global Assessment Report on Biodiversity and Ecosystems Services, the product of three years of work by 145 expert authors and another 310 contributors in 50 countries, the most comprehensive report of its kind ever produced, and certainly the most blunt. The report found that around 1 million animal and plant species are now threatened with extinction, many within decades, more than ever before in human history.

In the words of Assessment co-chair Professor Josef Settele, 'Ecosystems, species, wild populations, local varieties and breeds of domesticated plants and animals are shrinking, deteriorating or vanishing: The essential, interconnected web of life on Earth is getting smaller and increasingly frayed. This loss is a direct result of human activity and constitutes a direct threat to human well-being in all regions of the world.'[5]

The United Nations' summary of the report noted that 'global goals for conserving and sustainably using nature and achieving sustainability cannot be met by current trajectories'. The summary echoed IPBES chair Sir Robert Watson in stating, 'goals for 2030 and beyond may only be achieved through transformative changes across economic, social, political and technological factors ... Current negative trends in biodiversity and ecosystems will undermine progress towards 80 per cent of targets related to poverty, hunger, health, water, cities, climate, oceans and land. Loss of biodiversity is therefore shown to be not only an environmental issue, but also a developmental, economic, security, social and moral issue as well.'[6]

Parse those words. Rapid and far-reaching transitions ...

urban and infrastructure ... transformative changes ... economic, social, political and technological.

I opened this book with the declaration that the way we work today is no longer fit for human health and well-being or for the ideal productivity and profitability of industry. The truth is that every worker in extremis – stressed, overcommitted and mentally or physically unwell – is an individual embodiment of our entire planet. Now, the most conscientious students of its welfare have confirmed, beyond all doubt, that we must reinvent how we live, travel and work to survive as a species.

Back to the man on the couch with me outside the MPs' offices. If we follow his lead, we'll all go down with the cattle. On the other hand, if we take seriously the potential for transformative change of the four-day week and other productivity-driven models of flexibility in work, we might have a chance of saving our planet and all who live upon it.

After all – what have we got to lose?

Appendix: Qualitative Research by Dr Helen Delaney

Note: The following quotes are taken from conversations with Perpetual Guardian employees at the conclusion of the four-day week trial. Where the person quoted is in a managerial role, that is noted.

Table 1: Improvements in workplace dynamics

Theme	Supporting Evidence
Intellectual engagement and stimulation	'We were just testing out what's the most effective way to test how we measure our productivity and our work output. So we had quite a good discussion about how that works, and got our minds working – we never had to do this before, how do we begin this?'
	'I was so conscious about any duplications or inefficiencies in the work processes that in that trial period I made a whole list of anything that was taking extra time. My starting point is thought-provoking because it has caused our team to be reflective about how we approach our tasks and how to reallocate them or do them better.'

'Work smarter' innovations	'The way that we improved our turnaround time was by trying to automate it . . . So we've created formulas that input data a lot faster, so typing it out is all actually automated. That's sped up a lot of time. That was something we wanted to do, but obviously this trial made it happen.'
	'We looked at everything we did really and said do we need to be doing this, is this productive, should we be doing it at all, should someone else be doing it? We questioned everything we were doing . . .'
	'So what came through from the trial was particularly my focus around what does the business expect of me, and am I doing the tasks to progress that? My days are now filled up with client meetings, which is what they always should've been, but I was being distracted by other things.'
Collaboration and teamwork	'More collaborative, so the way my team is set up, we do quite individual roles, but we'd have to kind of work collaboratively to figure out how we can overlap and help each other out.'
	'I found the overriding thing was I was more impressed with the collaboration and teamwork within my team. They reprioritised their schedules and time to make sure that they met those pressing external obligations. They did that well, and then pulled in other staff members, who were definitely willing and wanting to engage and facilitated in helping. So I was genuinely really impressed with the level of collaboration and teamwork I saw. And a lot of that, mainly because it didn't have to be micromanaged or pushed for.'
	'Everyone seems to plan more now than they did before we started the trial . . . even I'm planning better than I did before, and I think generally our teams planned better, and they're planning within their pods or their teams as well. And it makes sure that they're not dropping the ball.'

Theme	Supporting Evidence
Delegation, sharing and trust	'It's like you want to delegate, because when you are away and you have to rely on your buddy, or other team members, to make sure the work that comes through will get done. And with the large portfolio that I have and the complexities, I've been reluctant in the past to just give it to others. But I've found that I've trained them, they know where to find what, and I was a lot more trusting in them. And things did get done, so I'm now more relaxed.'
	'I've got a great team around me who are really motivated, great client ethic, work well together, care about what they do. And so that helps me to be able to take that [gifted] day. And because of having that day, it means that they've got stronger relationships within the company and that sort of thing. It's not down to me having those relationships, so it means they get a chance to be able to move their careers and be the person.'
Upskilling, task variety	'With the client manager having a day off during the week, I probably got a bit more of a variety of the workload. I got to do new things and try new things which normally he would just do himself. I suppose now that we've gone back to the five-day work week and he's back doing those jobs, he doesn't feel the need to sort of pass them on. So it's limited a bit more of the learning for me.'
	'It made us expand how we worked and how we delegated the different levels of work. And I suppose I got to probably do more variety of activities because there were more time constraints and more pressure, so we found it quite exciting.'

Voice and empowerment	'We were all empowered to come up with the solution. The trial focused us on our team meetings and made sure that everybody had a bigger opportunity to speak. And we noticed that towards the end of the [trial], and even when we talked about the feedback that we want to put forward, everybody had something to say and contribute to the meetings.' 'I mean, you've even got the client assistant seeing clients. It's that simple thing, if they're not sure they'll come out and ask or whatever, but they're confident, or it's given them the confidence to go out and see clients that they weren't [seeing before].'
Focus and presence	'One of the things I noticed we did was instead of, say, doing half an hour of this, half an hour of that and you'd bounce from one job to the other, as I know I did, I put in three hours or two and a half hours just to do this one specific task. It put me in the mindset that that was what I was doing right there and then, and nothing else really mattered unless it was urgent.' 'I got through a lot more work in a shorter amount of time if I was dedicated to one task over two and a half hours. I just got stuck in and I did that with a few things, and I know one of the client managers did that as well, and it seemed to burn through the work real quick, which was great.' 'It's having that focus, that you're constantly thinking, right, I've got all of these things to do, this is my to-do list, I've got to get this done by Thursday night. And then you just get your head down and you get there and do it.'

Theme	Supporting Evidence
Goodwill and reciprocity	'The reward of the company giving back to you. And just the feeling that you're working somewhere that actually cares about your well-being and having co-workers that care about your life I think makes a big difference.'
	'If I was learning someone else's responsibilities then equally they were learning mine. So I didn't think for a minute, I'm doing extra work. I was just thinking we're helping each other.'
	'I think from the culture perspective it was just so much more energised and people really starting to move away from that [stance of], "This is my day job, this is boring, I come to work because I need a pay cheque. At the end of the day I don't find it that exciting, but wow, look at this opportunity that Andrew has given us." I really believe that there were a lot of people who genuinely felt, "What can I do to give back?"'
Stamina and motivation	'If I had to do a few emails, a few phone calls, take a few phone calls, it didn't worry me. I was still doing what I wanted to do, so that was quite okay.'
	'Coming back on a Thursday, you find the energy levels by Friday are still at a higher level than during the five-day week.'
	'I used to think, oh gosh, you know, only four days this week, that's great, then I get a three-day weekend and it just gives you that extra bit of oomph to get there.'

Organisational resilience, reduced risk	'We had the massive storm in Auckland on a Tuesday night and for the Wednesday it was really disruptive for the city of Auckland because people couldn't get into work or they had to deal with their electricity being off. But because we had so many of our staff away on a Wednesday and so many contingencies already in place for that particular day, I wonder if we came through it rather well. So from a business continuity planning perspective, I think this whole planning, and it's good for the city as well, keeps us off the streets.'
	'I was actually putting my hand up as the team leader of two people going, "You've got key person risk. Because one person knows how to do everything and it's all new processes and if he's sick for a week or if he takes his annual leave or whatever, none of you know how to do it."
	'It was important transactional stuff for the business. The great thing is, out of the trial, they all started communicating with how to do things and what to do and how to do it better and, on the day before he was off, he'd always debrief people at the end of the day about where things were at. He'd put it up on the whiteboard, client by client, of what needed to be done the next day. It gave me, as just an outside observer, so much more comfort in the fact that there was a lot less risk in that team because they were starting to work together a lot better.'

Table 2: Challenges and frustrations

Theme	Supporting Evidence
Stress and pressure	'You're squeezing so much into four days that you do feel like, or they felt like, the stress was definitely up.'
	'You're kind of making up for that day [off], but you're also often covering for someone else as well. And I saw that manifest itself in heightened stress levels in some of my direct reports.'
	'We didn't really make any [changes to how the team works]. I think it was just about kind of trying to cram all this work into the four days, which was difficult.'
	'The frustrations of having to wait [for information from another department/person]. And when you get information, I think the quality of some of the information that came through deteriorated during the trial. I think people were rushing things, they were trying to jam 100 per cent into 80 per cent and I think the quality suffered as a result of that. That includes communications with clients, which is where we generate our revenue.' (Manager report)

Workload incompatible with mandatory four-day work week	'The first day that I took off, I worked all day from home … I was checking emails and dealing with emails because I just didn't want to come back the next day and have to deal with all of that again.' (Manager report)
	'We found a lot of us weren't doing 32 hours, we're doing more … for this to work on a 32-hour work week we're going to need resourcing.'
	'We actually didn't reduce our working hours, because we came in earlier. We think we are pretty lean in the event and we just don't waste eight hours of time during the week. Also we had a little bit of a different situation because we'd lost a staff member, we lost a current manager and a current assistant and so we were having to cover their work as well in addition to everything else. So we just came in earlier, we did longer hours. We all felt that we'd be happy to do 12-hour days to have the fifth day off.'
	'Teams have said that they don't feel that with their current workloads it's actually workable to continue with it. But they said they can see a rolling four days, five days, four days, five days as something that is more achievable. So they came up with that themselves. They said, we feel like we got behind, and I could see that they were definitely stressed in some cases. And they said, I'm actually going to come in on half of my day off tomorrow because I need to.'

Theme	Supporting Evidence
Skill variation	'I guess [the trial] showed there were a lot of skill gaps between tasks, which certain team members couldn't do within our team … because of the short notice of the trial it was a bit of a rush to put those skills together so that those skills were available during those days.'
	'Everyone is very reliant on [my manager] because she's got a huge skill set … So she definitely would have worked beyond her four-day week, even though it would have been from home. But there was no possible way that it couldn't, but they learned that that's an upskilling opportunity going forward.'
Perceived attitudinal differences	'What I observed was variable behaviours among team members. Some people were emotionally invested into it and would change their work habits accordingly, whereas others took it as a gift and didn't change.' (Manager report)
Perceived lack of significant innovation	'My team told me they had different behavioural changes, so each said they were more focused, maybe more energised. Personally, I didn't notice any difference. But nothing slipped. No one slacked off, nothing slipped. But I didn't see a drive, I didn't see busyness, I didn't see, ooh, how are we going to do this better and more innovative? There were no new initiatives so that was a bit of a disappointment, because I did challenge them to think that way.' (Manager report)

Table 3: Impact of reduced working hours on non-work lives

Theme	Supporting Evidence
Time to participate in family life	'It enabled more time with my kids. I've got three school-age children, so I was able to do the lunchtime sausage sizzle, which I normally wouldn't get the opportunity to do because I'm at work. I was also able to be involved in pet day and catch my children's softball final. Those kind of things that I don't normally get a chance to be involved in . . . [My kids] absolutely loved it . . . they're like, "Oh, you're always at work, you never come to our things." So having me there was a real boost for them.'
	'I was at playcentre with the four-year-old. It was a unique environment, I don't normally see him in that . . . and being one of the only dads that goes into the environment. So all the other mothers really liked it because it was different, there were some different ways of playing and that type of thing.'
	'I spent one day with my husband, went out for lunch, a weekday lunch – how great is that? Something that we never normally have an opportunity [to do].'
	'On the weekend, on Saturday you do your washing and you clean your house, you do everything. You could do that on the Friday and then actually on a Saturday and Sunday you had them free. And you could actually relax and think, now I can spend some good quality time with friends and family. But it was nice just to have a "you" day, which you don't have much because it's rush, rush, rush in the week- ends. I suppose it just gives you that, you make more of an effort to spend time with people you probably wouldn't so much in the weekends, like grandparents.'
	'We saved a bit of money being able to pick up the kids ourselves and not having to pay the nanny.'

Theme	Supporting Evidence
Time to accomplish tasks	'The days off have been busy, but have been like good busy, things I've wanted to do but I couldn't get to because I was at work.'
	'The three days is really productive personally as well. So overall you just feel good generally.'
	'Just get time to do things you wouldn't otherwise have done. I did all the washing on the Friday so the wife didn't have to do it on Saturday, so she was much happier with me and therefore happier with the kids. And therefore everybody was happier. There's that, I don't know what it is, endorphins or euphoria or something that gets released when you do a job and you know you've done it well and finished it.'

Time to restore and reconnect	'And one day, it was a guilty pleasure, I spent time by myself. No husband, no kids, pure indulgence, just me, myself and I. It was just so good.'
	'Things come to you on your day off that wouldn't come to you when you're sitting at your desk … It's that head space, it's that ability to think.'
	'Also time to just reflect a bit and be quiet, and recharge your batteries. Because [while] some people get energy and recharge by being with people, I need to be alone. We're all different. And when you're with people all day and sometimes you've got so much to do, you need some time to just chill out, uninterrupted time. So that was huge for me.'
	'I'm not a morning person, so mornings are stressful between the traffic, hitting the snooze button half a dozen times, et cetera. So when I could I started [work] around 10, the odd days when I had meetings, so I'd start later. But I enjoyed that because I'd come in and I was less stressed, so I'd catch the bus rather than driving. So I saved some money on transport costs. The odd days I went for a walk and went for a coffee in my neighbourhood rather than racing over the road. Had the odd snooze, which was a proper sleep-in without hitting the snooze button.'

Theme	Supporting Evidence
	'I do all the community activities as well. So that off day gave me some more time to focus and make sure it does get completed around that time.'
Time to learn and contribute	'I found that that extra day in the week I could be really productive in my volunteer work, because I can get so much done. So my day off was Thursday because I study two papers as well at university and Thursday is the day I have classes … Afterwards I'd be able to either hang out with some friends or I'd be able to go home early and then relax. Most of my friends are still all at university, so it was good for me to be able to catch up with them because sometimes I feel like I miss out on actually being at university. And I got to go to some of the speakers' events the law school organises, which was a really good experience, because I normally wouldn't have time to go to them.'
Time to explore and imagine	'Someone said to me, now you've got at least 48 extra days in your life every year, imagine if it went forward, what are you going to do with that? That was just a passing comment from someone but it keeps ringing in my ear and I keep thinking to myself, What am I going to do? What could I do for me? So every day of the trial, I went to a new fitness class – completely new to me, I'd never been to this gym before.'

Acknowledgements

Given this was, in many ways, an accidental journey from a slightly crazy idea to a global movement, I have a lot of people to thank.

First, to my partner Charlotte for her love, support, suggestions (the elimination of 'that' throughout the book is the least of her many achievements) and encouragement throughout the writing of the book. The development of the global four-day week campaign has been a great journey to go on together.

To Stephanie Jones, this book could not have been written without you. Thanks for working with my wilder ideas and for your exhaustive research of the world of flexible working. You helped turn theory into reality.

To the whole team at Perpetual Guardian, especially Christine Brotherton. Thank you for taking up the idea of the four-day week and making it such a success. Special thanks to Tammy, Kirsten, Marina, Willem and Cleo for sharing how the four-day week affected you personally. Apologies for the intrusion, but it made the story so real for so many.

To Kate, Dwayne and the whole team at Alexander PR, you did an incredible job in getting the story out and fielding enquiries from all over the world, at all times and with such professionalism and good humour.

To Associate Professor Jarrod Haar and Dr Helen Delaney, your research was integral in giving the Perpetual Guardian trial such credibility in the global arena. Thanks also to the editors of the *Guardian* and the *New York Times*, whose interest turned this into the global story it has become.

Thank you to Tom Asker and the team at Little, Brown for your help, encouragement and patience in getting this book over the line!

Finally, and importantly, thank you to all the companies and individuals who have reached out and joined the journey to implement a four-day week. Together we are making the world a better and healthier place, one company at a time.

Bibliography

Alderman, Liz, 'France moves to tax tech giants, stoking fight with White House', NYtimes.com, 11 July 2019

Armstrong, Ashley, 'What's the real cost to society of a £5 dress?', Telegraph.co.uk, 15 January 2019

Arnold, Sara, 'The first step to starting your career in sustainable fashion', businessoffashion.com, 11 October 2018

Arnold, Sarah, 'Stressed economy, stressed society, stressed NHS', Neweconomics.org, 18 May 2018

Batchelor, Sandy, 'Telecommuting for the planet', climatechange.ucdavis.edu, 6 September 2018

Bennet, Sydney, 'Rise of the super commuters', Apartmentlist.com, 24 April 2018

Bloom, Nick, Kretschmer, Tobias and Van Reenen, John, 'Work-life balance, management practices, and productivity', NBER.org, September 2009

Brown, John Murray, 'UK self-employed plumber wins court battle for workers' rights', FT.com, 11 February 2017

Calfas, Jennifer, 'Meet the CEO whose comments about mental health in the workplace went viral', Money.com, 11 July 2017

Chang, Emily, *Brotopia: Breaking Up the Boys' Club of Silicon Valley*, Portfolio, 2018

Chapman, Ben, 'Uber drivers are entitled to workers' rights, Court of Appeal says in landmark gig economy ruling', Independent.co.uk, 19 December 2018

Chazan, Guy, 'German union wins right to 28-hour working week and 4.3% pay rise', FT.com, 7 February 2018

Chu, Ben, 'What is productivity? And why does it matter that it is falling again?', Independent.co.uk, 6 October 2017

Congress (US), *Invest in Women, Invest in America: A Comprehensive Review of Women in the U.S. Economy*, Congress (US) Joint Economic Committee, December 2010

Day, Meagan, 'The fraud and the four-hour workweek', Jacobinmag.com, 27 March 2018

Denning, Steve, 'What is agile?', Forbes.com, 13 August 2016

Elliott, Larry, 'Economics: whatever happened to Keynes' 15-hour working week?', TheGuardian.com, 1 September 2008

Evans, Lisa, 'The exact amount of time you should work every day', FastCompany.com, 15 September 2014

Fleishman, Glenn, 'New York makes Uber and Lyft pay a $17.22 an hour minimum plus expenses to their drivers', Fortune.com, 4 December 2018

Fleming, Peter, 'Do you work more than 39 hours a week? Your job could be killing you', TheGuardian.com, 15 January 2018

Fowler, Susan, '"What have we done?" Silicon Valley engineers fear they've created a monster', VanityFair.com, 9 August 2018

Fremstad, Anders, Paul, Mark and Underwood, Anthony, 'Work hours and CO_2 emissions: evidence from U.S. households', TandFonline.com, 27 June 2019

Frier, Sarah, 'How Sheryl Sandberg's sharing manifesto drives Facebook', Bloomberg.com, 27 April 2017

Griffey, Harriet, 'The lost art of concentration: being distracted in a digital world', TheGuardian.com, 14 October 2018

Griffith, Erin, 'Are young people pretending to love work?', NYtimes.com, 26 January 2019

Hanauer, Nick, 'The pitchforks are coming ... for us plutocrats', Politico.com, July/August 2014

Henderson, Tim, 'In most states, a spike in "super
    commuters"', The Associated Press via Pewtrusts.org,
    5 June 2017

Hook, Leslie, 'Year in a word: gig economy', FT.com,
    30 December 2015

Huberman, Michael and Minns, Chris, 'The times they are not
    changin': Days and hours of work in Old and New Worlds,
    1870–2000', *Explorations in Economic History*, 12 July 2007

Huggler, Justin, 'German workers win right to 28-hour
    working week', Telegraph.co.uk, 7 February 2018

Hultman, Nathan and Bodnar, Paul, 'Trump tried to kill the
    Paris agreement, but the effect has been the opposite',
    brookings.edu, 1 June 2018

Hymas, Charles, 'A decade of smartphones: We now spend an
    entire day every week online', Telegraph.co.uk, 2 August
    2018

Imber, Amanda, 'Why you are losing 10 IQ points every time
    this happens', entrepreneur.com, 19 February 2018

Judge, T.A., Thoresen, C.J., Bono, J.E., Patton, G.K. (2001), 'The
    job satisfaction–job performance relationship: A qualitative
    and quantitative review', *Psychological Bulletin*, 127, 376–407

Lyons, Dan, *Lab Rats: How Silicon Valley Made Work Miserable
    for the Rest of Us*, Hachette Book Group, 2018

MacKay, Jory, 'Managing interruptions at work: what we
    learned surveying hundreds of RescueTime users about
    their worst distractions', Blog.RescueTime.com, 29 May 2018

Matousek, Mark, 'Elon Musk says you need to work at least 80
    hours a week to change the world', inc.com, 27 November
    2018

Matthews, Dylan, 'Are 26 billionaires worth more than half the
    planet? The debate, explained', Vox.com, 22 January 2019

Maxwell, Diane, 'Diane Maxwell: politics is downstream from
    culture', Stuff.co.nz, 29 December 2016

McGregor, Jena, 'The average work week is now 47 hours',
    Washingtonpost.com, 2 September 2014

Miller, Lee J. and Lu, Wei, 'Housing prices are through the
    roof in these 10 cities', Bloomberg.com, 5 October 2018

Moore, Heidi, 'New study proves it really is harder to find a
    job as you get older', Theladders.com, 28 February 2017

Murphy, Mark, 'Interruptions at work are killing your
    productivity', Forbes.com, 30 October 2016

Murray, Sarah, 'The internet restriction apps that help improve
    productivity', TheGuardian.com, 17 December 2014

Neate, Rupert, 'Amazon's Jeff Bezos pays out $38bn in divorce
    settlement', TheGuardian.com, 30 June 2019

O'Connor, Sarah, 'Dark factories: labour exploitation in
    Britain's garment industry', FT.com, 17 May 2018

Pellegrino, Nicky, 'How the rise in workplace depression
    and anxiety is causing job culture to change', Noted.co.nz,
    25 September 2017

Powis, Joanna, 'Supreme Court decision announced in Pimlico
    Plumbers case', Employmentlawwatch.com, 14 June 2018

Pullar-Strecker, Tom, 'Spark employment move "a recipe for
    disaster", says expert', Stuff.co.nz, 14 June 2018

Pullar-Strecker, Tom, 'Vodafone goes Agile but says staff
    won't have to sign new contracts', Stuff.co.nz, 19 July 2018

Rasmussen, Peter, 'Hard-selling – recruitment joke', LinkedIn.
    com, 18 November 2014

Reaney, Patricia, 'U.S. workers spend 6.3 hours a day checking
    email: survey', Huffpost.com, 26 August 2015

Sanghani, Radhika, 'What happened when I rented my
    wardrobe for a week', Telegraph.co.uk, 23 April 2019

Schaefer, Annette, 'Commuting takes its toll',
    ScientificAmerican.com, 1 October 2005

Schwab, Klaus, 'The Fourth Industrial Revolution: what it
    means, how to respond', Weforum.org, 14 January 2016

Scott, Sophie and Armitage, Rebecca, 'Why your job might be making you sick', ABC.net.au, 11 May 2018

Semuels, Alana, 'What happens when gig-economy workers become employees', TheAtlantic.com, 14 September 2018

Son, Sabrina, 'How social exchange theory applies to the workplace', tinypulse.com, 1 March 2016

Stevens, Tony, 'Mental health days need to be taken seriously', Stuff.co.nz, 31 July 2018

Stock, Rob, 'KiwiSaver contribution "holidays" to get shorter', Stuff.co.nz, 2 July 2018

Stroup, Caitlin and Yoon, Joy, 'What impact do flexible working arrangements (FWA) have on employee performance and overall business results?', Cornell University, ILR School site: digitalcommons.ilr.cornell.edu, 2016

Thompson, Derek, 'A formula for perfect productivity: work for 52 minutes, break for 17', TheAtlantic.com, 17 September 2014

Tsang, Amie and Satariano, Adam, 'Apple to add $1 billion campus in Austin, Tex., in broad U.S. hiring push', NYtimes.com, 13 December 2018

Turner, Giles, 'How big tech will be hit by U.K.'s new digital tax', Bloomberg.com, 30 October 2018

Umoh, Ruth, 'Here's what working 120 hours a week like Elon Musk really does to the body and the mind', CNBC.com, 22 August 2018

Usher, Pip, 'Digital detoxes: do they really work?', Vogue.co.uk, 1 May 2018

Wall, Matthew, 'Smartphone stress: Are you a victim of "always on" culture?', BBC.com, 14 August 2014

Wallace-Wells, David, 'Jared Diamond: there's a 49 percent chance the world as we know it will end by 2050', NYmag.com, 10 May 2019

Wei, Marlynn, 'Commuting: "The stress that doesn't pay"',
    Psychologytoday.com, 12 January 2015
Williamson, Lucy, 'France's Macron brings back national
    service', BBC.com, 27 June 2018
Wilson, Josh, 'Work-related stress and mental illness now
    accounts for over half of work absences', Telegraph.co.uk,
    1 November 2018
Young, Molly, 'Don't distract me', NYtimes.com, 26 January
    2019
Zarya, Valentina, 'Working flexible hours can hurt your
    career – but only if you're a woman', Fortune.com,
    21 February 2017
Ziffer, Daniel, '"Hump day" killed off, app maker Versa's
    staff repay the box with higher productivity', ABC.net.au,
    17 April 2019
'21 hours: the case for a shorter working week',
    NewEconomics.org, 13 February 2010
'After drawing a line under layoffs, Vodafone NZ boss Jason
    Paris faces five challenges', NZHerald.co.nz, 1 April 2019
'An IPCC Special Report on the impacts of global warming
    of 1.5°C above pre-industrial levels and related global
    greenhouse gas emission pathways, in the context of
    strengthening the global response to the threat of climate
    change, sustainable development, and efforts to eradicate
    poverty - Headline Statements from the Summary for
    Policymakers', ipcc.ch
'Benefits from Auckland road decongestion', EMA.co.nz,
    10 July 2017
'Champions of the gig economy', BBC.com
'Doing better for families', OECD.org, 2011
'Employer need » Increased cost savings & profits',
    Sloan Center on Aging & Work at Boston College,
    workplaceflexibility.bc.edu

'Employment Relations Act 2000', legislation.govt.nz

'Flexible working to contribute $10tr to global economy by 2030', menaherald.com, 17 October 2018

'FOUR – What is it good for? A study of the four-day week: a report by The Mix', 2018

'Four Better or Four Worse?', Henley Business School, University of Reading, 2019

'Four-day week pays off for UK business', Henley Business School, University of Reading, henley.ac.uk, 3 July 2019

'Gender pay gap in the UK: 2018', ONS.gov.uk

'Gender wage gap', Data.oecd.org

'Getting your super started – employees', ATO.gov.au

'Global real house price index', Global Housing Watch, IMF. com

'Hours worked', Data.oecd.org

'How many productive hours in a work day? Just 2 hours, 23 minutes . . . ', Vouchercloud.com

'How the tech industry changed our work culture', RNZ. co.nz, 11 March 2019

'Impress me: how to make your first job count', RNZ.co.nz, 9 November 2018

'Is the traditional 9-5 working week finally dead?', HCAmag. com, 14 June 2018

'Ma Yun talks 996' https://mp.weixin.qq.com/s/ oc0NugBjpsn1_mBtbib2Lg

'Mental health in the workplace', WHO.int, May 2019

'School may build houses to stop teachers fleeing Auckland's high housing costs', NZherald.com, 3 June 2017

'Spark announces leadership team changes as part of move to Agile', Sparknz.co.nz, 12 March 2018

'The new work order', The Foundation for Young Australians, 2014

'The Schedules that Work Act of 2017', warren.senate.gov

'The tight labour market is making unskilled work more
    unpredictable', Economist.com, 8 December 2018
'UK employees work longer hours than most EU
    neighbours', BBC.com, 8 December 2011
'What is social exchange theory?', socialwork.tulane.edu,
    20 April 2018
'Work related stress depression or anxiety statistics in Great
    Britain, 2018', HSE.gov.uk, 31 October 2018
'Work-life balance and the economics of workplace
    flexibility', Executive Office of the President Council of
    Economic Advisers, Cornell University, LIR School site:
    digitalcommons.ilr.cornell.edu, 2010
'Work', TED.com
Definition of 'gig', Collinsdictionary.com
DHL-CarbonCalculator.com
https://bcorporation.net/about-b-corps
https://www.anxiety.org.nz/
Submission from Volunteering New Zealand on the
    discussion paper 'Quality Flexible Work', Volunteeringnz.
    org.nz

Notes

Introduction

1. https://economictimes.indiatimes.com/jobs/india-inc-looks-to-deal-with-rising-stress-in-employees/articleshow/64741313.cms?from=mdr; https://www.workforce.com/2018/11/17/millennials-in-india-lead-as-the-most-stressed-in-the-world/; http://www.chinadaily.com.cn/a/201811/02/WS5bdbdf4ca310eff303286339.html; http://www.chinadaily.com.cn/china/2016-12/11/content_27635578.htm

Chapter One: The World of Work As It Is Today

1. https://personal.lse.ac.uk/minns/Huberman_Minns_EEH_2007.pdf
2. https://www.ft.com/content/e7f0490e-0b1c-11e8-8eb7-42f857ea9f09
3. https://stats.oecd.org/Index.aspx?DataSetCode=ANHRS

4. https://www.bbc.com/news/business-16082186
5. https://www.washingtonpost.com/news/on-leadership/wp/2014/09/02/the-average-work-week-is-now-47-hours/?utm_term=.1b6cfd88dc62
6. https://www.fya.org.au/wp-content/uploads/2015/08/fya-future-of-work-report-final-lr.pdf
7. https://www.theladders.com/career-advice/new-study-proves-it-is-harder-to-find-a-job-as-you-get-older
8. https://www.huffingtonpost.com/entry/check-work-email-hours-survey_us_55ddd168e4b0a40aa3ace672
9. https://www.telegraph.co.uk/news/2018/08/01/decade-smartphones-now-spend-entire-day-every-week-online/
10. https://www.bbc.com/news/business-28686235
11. https://www.bloomberg.com/news/features/2017-04-27/how-sheryl-sandberg-s-sharing-manifesto-drives-facebook
12. https://www.oecd.org/els/family/47701118.pdf
13. Ibid., p.24.
14. Ibid., p.29.
15. Ibid., p.30.
16. Ibid., p.36.
17. https://www.independent.co.uk/news/business/analysis-and-features/productivity-what-is-it-meaning-define-uk-economy-explained-a7986781.html
18. https://www.vouchercloud.com/resources/office-worker-productivity
19. Ibid.
20. https://www.imf.org/external/research/housing/
21. https://www.nzherald.co.nz/nz/news/article.cfm?c_id=1&objectid=11868150
22. https://www.bloomberg.com/news/

articles/2018-10-04/home-cost-index-says-ouch-hong-kong-oh-canada-hello-dubai

23. https://www.apartmentlist.com/rentonomics/
increase-in-long-super-commutes/

24. https://www.pewtrusts.org/en/research-and-analysis/blogs/stateline/2017/06/05/in-most-states-a-spike-in-super-commuters

25. https://www.scientificamerican.com/article/commuting-takes-its-toll/

26. Ibid.

27. Ibid.

28. Ibid.

29. https://www.psychologytoday.com/intl/blog/urban-survival/201501/commuting-the-stress-doesnt-pay

30. https://www.bbc.com/news/business-28686235

31. https://www.telegraph.co.uk/news/2018/11/01/work-related-stress-mental-illness-now-accounts-half-work-absences/

32. https://neweconomics.org/2018/05/stressed-economy-stressed-society-stressed-nhs

33. https://www.pressreader.com/new-zealand/new-zealand-listener/20170901/281535111129140

34. https://www.who.int/mental_health/in_the_workplace/en/

35. https://www.abc.net.au/news/2018-05-11/why-your-job-might-be-making-you-sick/9747518

Chapter Two: The Workers' Response

1. https://www.radionz.co.nz/national/programmes/afternoons/audio/2018686029/how-the-tech-industry-changed-our-work-culture

2. Ibid.
3. https://www.nytimes.com/2019/01/26/business/
    against-hustle-culture-rise-and-grind-tgim.html
4. https://www.nytimes.com/2016/01/31/books/
    review/dont-distract-me.html
5. Ibid.
6. https://www.ted.com/topics/work
7. https://www.vogue.co.uk/article/
    digital-detox-results
8. https://www.theguardian.com/
    small-business-network/2014/dec/17/
    internet-restriction-apps-productivity
9. https://jacobinmag.com/2018/03/
    four-hour-workweek-tim-ferriss-work
10. http://money.com/money/4853305/mental-health-
    workplace-olark-madalyn-parker-ben-congleton/
11. https://www.stuff.co.nz/life-style/
    well-good/105881646/mental-health-days-need-to-be-
    taken-seriously#comments
12. Ibid.
13. https://www.ft.com/
    content/259618fe-ef87-11e6-ba01-119a44939bb6
14. https://www.employmentlawwatch.com/2018/06/
    articles/employment-uk/supreme-court-decision-
    announced-in-pimlico-plumbers-case/
15. https://www.independent.co.uk/news/business/
    news/uber-drivers-workers-rights-case-court-of-
    appeal-gig-economy-ruling-a8691026.html
16. https://www.dhl-carboncalculator.com/#/
    scenarios

Chapter Three: The Corporate Response

1. https://www.weforum.org/agenda/2016/01/
   the-fourth-industrial-revolution-what-it-means-and-how-
   to-respond
2. https://www.politico.com/magazine/story/2014/06/
   the-pitchforks-are-coming-for-us-plutocrats-108014
3. https://www.collinsdictionary.com/dictionary/english/
   gig
4. https://www.ft.com/content/
   b5a2b122-a41b-11e5-8218-6b8ff73aae15
5. https://www.theatlantic.com/
   technology/archive/2018/09/
   gig-economy-independent-contractors/570307/
6. https://www.vanityfair.com/news/2018/08/
   silicon-valley-engineers-fear-they-created-a-monster
7. http://fortune.com/2018/12/04/
   uber-lyft-via-drivers-minimum-wage-nyc/
8. https://www.radionz.co.nz/programmes/
   two-cents-worth/story/2018670560/
   impress-me-how-to-make-your-first-job-count
9. http://www.bbc.com/storyworks/capital/
   the-rise-of-the-free-agent/champions-of-the-gig-economy
10. https://www.economist.com/
    united-states/2018/12/08/the-tight-labour-market-is-
    making-unskilled-work-more-predictable
11. Chang. *Brotopia: Breaking Up the Boys' Club of Silicon
    Valley*, p. 211.
12. https://www.vanityfair.com/news/2018/08/
    silicon-valley-engineers-fear-they-created-a-monster
13. https://www.nytimes.com/2018/12/13/business/apple-
    austin-campus.html?action=click&module=Top%20
    Stories&pgtype=Homepage

14. https://www.bloomberg.com/news/articles/2018-10-29/how-big-tech-will-be-hit-by-u-k-s-new-digital-tax-quicktake
15. https://www.nytimes.com/2019/07/11/business/france-digital-tax-tech-giants.html
16. https://www.politico.com/magazine/story/2014/06/the-pitchforks-are-coming-for-us-plutocrats-108014
17. https://www.vox.com/future-perfect/2019/1/22/18192774/oxfam-inequality-report-2019-davos-wealth
18. https://www.theguardian.com/technology/2019/jun/30/amazon-jeff-bezos-ex-wife-mackenzie-handed-38bn-in-divorce-settlement
19. *Brotopia*, p. 189.
20. https://www.forbes.com/sites/stevedenning/2016/08/13/what-is-agile/#745ce1ec26e3
21. Ibid.
22. https://www.sparknz.co.nz/news/Spark-announces-leadership-team-changes.html
23. https://www.stuff.co.nz/business/industries/105575857/vodafone-goes-agile-but-says-staff-wont-have-to-sign-new-contracts
24. https://www.nzherald.co.nz/business/news/article.cfm?c_id=3&objectid=12217900
25. https://www.stuff.co.nz/business/industries/105575857/vodafone-goes-agile-but-says-staff-wont-have-to-sign-new-contracts
26. https://www.stuff.co.nz/business/industries/104703350/spark-gives-staff-a-week-to-consider-new-job-contracts
27. https://www.forbes.com/sites/stevedenning/2016/08/13/what-is-agile/#745ce1ec26e3

Chapter Five: The Data

1. https://www.henley.ac.uk/fourdayweek
2. Ibid.
3. http://themixlondon.com/wp-content/uploads/2018/10/FOUR-What-Is-It-Good-For.pdf?utm_source=mailchimp&utm_campaign=03004ec1e1f0&utm_medium=page

Chapter Six: How It Is Done

1. https://blog.rescuetime.com/interruptions-at-work/
2. https://www.forbes.com/sites/markmurphy/2016/10/30/interruptions-at-work-are-killing-your-productivity/#62e68f461689
3. Ibid.
4. https://blog.rescuetime.com/interruptions-at-work/
5. https://www.forbes.com/sites/markmurphy/2016/10/30/interruptions-at-work-are-killing-your-productivity/#62e68f461689
6. https://www.nber.org/chapters/c0441.pdf, p17.
7. https://www.fastcompany.com/3035605/the-exact-amount-of-time-you-should-work-every-day
8. https://www.theatlantic.com/business/archive/2014/09/science-tells-you-how-many-minutes-should-you-take-a-break-for-work-17/380369/

Chapter 7: The Broader Benefits

1. https://neweconomics.org/2010/02/21-hours
2. https://www.ema.co.nz/resources/EMA%20Reports%20and%20Documents/Advocacy/Submissions/2017/NZIER%20report%20on%20

Auckland%20Benefits%20of%20Decongestion.pdf

3.   https://climatechange.ucdavis.edu/what-can-i-do/
      telecommuting-for-the-planet/
4.   Ibid.
5.   https://www.henley.ac.uk/news/2019/
      four-day-week-pays-off-for-uk-business
6.   https://www.tandfonline.com/doi/full/10.1080/0953
      8259.2019.1592950
7.   https://www.volunteeringnz.org.nz/wp-content/
      uploads/Quality-Flexible-Work-Submission.pdf
8.   https://socialwork.tulane.edu/blog/
      social-exchange-theory
9.   https://www.tinypulse.com/blog/
      sk-social-exchange-theory-in-the-workplace
10.   https://www.bbc.com/news/world-europe-44625625
11.   http://fortune.com/2017/02/21/
      flexible-schedule-women-career/
12.   Ibid.
13.   https://data.oecd.org/earnwage/gender-wage-gap.
      htm
14.   https://www.ons.gov.uk/
      employmentandlabourmarket/peopleinwork/
      earningsandworkinghours/bulletins/
      genderpaygapintheuk/2018
15.   http://www.hse.gov.uk/statistics/causdis/stress.pdf
16.   https://www.abc.net.au/news/2019-04-17/
      killing-hump-day-business-that-shuts-wednesdays-
      workers-happier/10985332

Chapter 8: The Importance of Being Flexible

1.   Dan Lyons, *Lab Rats: How Silicon Valley Made Work
      Miserable for the Rest of Us*, Hachette Book Group, 2018

2. https://books.google.co.nz/books?id=2Ek6k1mR3xgC&
pg=PA13&lpg=PA13&dq=deloitte+FWAs+$41.5+million
&source=bl&ots=TrKagbOZ9h&sig=gT552a7xA6e9ILEsF
kS4aIjIjF0&hl=en&sa=X&ved=2ahUKEwiw6uLdh6jfAhV
WOSsKHQaXAdEQ6AEwFXoECAoQAQ#v=onepage&q
=deloitte%20FWAs%20%2441.5%20million&f=false

3. https://digitalcommons.ilr.cornell.edu/cgi/viewcontent.
cgi?referer=https://www.google.com/&httpsredir=1&ar
ticle=1719&context=key_workplace

4. https://www.hcamag.com/nz/news/general/
is-the-traditional-9-5-working-week-finally-dead/152596

5. https://digitalcommons.ilr.cornell.edu/cgi/viewcontent.
cgi?referer=https://www.google.com/&httpsredir=1&ar
ticle=1121&context=student

6. Judge, T.A., Thoresen, C.J., Bono, J.E. and Patton, G.K.
(2001), 'The job satisfaction–job performance relationship:
A qualitative and quantitative review', *Psychological
Bulletin*, 127, 376–407

7. http://workplaceflexibility.bc.edu/need/
need_employers_cost

8. https://www.menaherald.com/
en/business/events-services/
flexible-working-contribute-10tr-global-economy-2030

9. https://www.stuff.co.nz/business/
opinion-analysis/87911259/
diane-maxwell-politics-is-downstream-from-culture

10. https://www.ato.gov.au/individuals/super/
getting-your-super-started/employees/

11. https://www.stuff.co.nz/business/money/105167852/
kiwisaver-contribution-holidays-to-get-shorter

12. https://www.anxiety.org.nz/; http://www.hse.gov.uk/
statistics/causdis/stress.pdf

Chapter 9: The Obstacles

1. http://www.legislation.govt.nz/act/public/2000/0024/
    latest/DLM6803000.html#DLM6803000
2. https://www.warren.senate.gov/files/
    documents/2017_06_20_STWA_Factsheet.pdf
3. https://www.ft.com/content/
    e7f0490e-0b1c-11e8-8eb7-42f857ea9f09
4. https://www.telegraph.co.uk/news/2018/02/07/
    german-workers-win-right-28-hour-working-week/
5. https://www.telegraph.co.uk/business/2019/01/15/
    real-cost-society-5-dress/
6. https://www.ft.com/content/
    e427327e-5892-11e8-b8b2-d6ceb45fa9d0
7. https://www.telegraph.co.uk/business/2019/01/15/
    real-cost-society-5-dress/
8. https://www.ft.com/content/
    e427327e-5892-11e8-b8b2-d6ceb45fa9d0
9. https://www.telegraph.co.uk/fashion/style/
    happened-rented-wardrobe-week/
10. https://www.businessoffashion.com/articles/opinion/
    op-ed-the-first-step-to-starting-your-career-in-
    sustainable-fashion?utm_campaign=0f23447e69-is-this-
    influencer-the-future-of-fashion&utm_medium=email&
    utm_source=Subscribers&utm_term=0_d2191372b3-
    0f23447e69-419286197&fbclid=IwAR1BacwEUg25w
    Ve2Cw0WvAKwxbfXSmyBuhT0KnJqfwCMWBf
    MMmMoxvbBvoM
11. https://bcorporation.net/about-b-corps

Chapter 10: Inside the Business Walls

1. https://mp.weixin.qq.com/s/ocONugBjpsn1_mBtbib2Lg
2. https://www.inc.com/business-insider/elon-musk-says-you-need-to-work-80-hours-a-week-to-save-the-world.html
3. https://www.cnbc.com/2018/08/22/what-working-120-hours-a-week-like-teslas-elon-musk-does-to-the-body.html
4. https://www.theguardian.com/lifeandstyle/2018/jan/15/is-28-hours-ideal-working-week-for-healthy-life
5. https://www.cnbc.com/2018/08/22/what-working-120-hours-a-week-like-teslas-elon-musk-does-to-the-body.html
6. https://www.theguardian.com/lifeandstyle/2018/oct/14/the-lost-art-of-concentration-being-distracted-in-a-digital-world
7. https://www.entrepreneur.com/article/309039
8. https://www.vouchercloud.com/resources/office-worker-productivity

Conclusion: Cows Need Milking Twice a Day

1. https://www.theguardian.com/business/2008/sep/01/economics
2. http://nymag.com/intelligencer/2019/05/jared-diamond-on-his-new-book-upheaval.html
3. https://www.brookings.edu/blog/planetpolicy/2018/06/01/trump-tried-to-kill-the-paris-agreement-but-the-effect-has-been-the-opposite/
4. https://www.ipcc.ch/site/assets/uploads/sites/2/2018/07/sr15_headline_statements.pdf
5. https://www.un.org/sustainabledevelopment/blog/2019/05/nature-decline-unprecedented-report/
6. Ibid.